IMAGES
of America

PISECO LAKE AND ARIETTA

Piseco Lake (pronounced *pi-SEE-ko*) is located in Hamilton County in the township of Arietta. The spectacular panoramic views have attracted visitors to this awe-inspiring southern Adirondack lake for generations. As 19th-century resident Ephraim Phillips once stated, "This lake is deservingly regarded as one of the most beautiful sheets of water in the Adirondack Wilderness." Over 100 years later, many still agree.

On the cover: Please see page 41. (Courtesy of the Piseco Lake Historical Society.)

IMAGES
of America

PISECO LAKE AND ARIETTA

Frederick T. Adcock and Cynthia E. Adcock

ARCADIA
PUBLISHING

Copyright © 2008 by Frederick T. Adcock and Cynthia E. Adcock
ISBN 978-1-5316-3487-2

Published by Arcadia Publishing
Charleston, South Carolina

Library of Congress Catalog Card Number: 2007927924

For all general information contact Arcadia Publishing at:
Telephone 843-853-2070
Fax 843-853-0044
E-mail sales@arcadiapublishing.com
For customer service and orders:
Toll-Free 1-888-313-2665

Visit us on the Internet at www.arcadiapublishing.com

Visible in this unique 1920s aerial photograph is nearly every notable feature of Piseco Lake. The lake covers an area of 2,842 acres and encompasses over 20 miles of shoreline. With an elevation of 1,661 feet, this body of water is approximately seven miles long and two miles wide, with the greatest depth extending 129 feet. Known for its abundance of lake trout and whitefish, Piseco Lake has been a popular destination for anglers for over 150 years.

CONTENTS

ACKNOWLEDGMENTS

The authors convey sincere thanks to the Piseco Lake Historical Society and all of the individuals who have donated historically significant materials to the organization that were invaluable to the content of this book. Our gratitude extends to Lee and Lynne Billington, whose time and dedication have revived much interest in preserving the local history of the Piseco area. A special thanks to Bill and Roberta Abrams, Rick Higgins, the Blessing family, the Ackerman family, and the Liddell family for sharing personal photographs and stories of experiences at Piseco Lake, which complemented the authors' extensive postcard collections. The late Frank Rix is also acknowledged for the legacy he has left future generations through his unique photographic images of the Piseco area.

We are grateful to Steven N. Nassiff for his artistic renderings, which were essential to complete the story of Piseco Lake in the absence of historical photographs. We kindly thank Philip A. Nassiff, Esq., for his expertise and assistance with literary legalities encountered while writing *Piseco Lake and Arietta*.

Any persons interested in further readings in regard to Piseco Lake are strongly encouraged to delve into the books *The History of Hamilton County* by Ted Aber and Stella King and the *Sesquicentennial of the Town of Arietta*.

This book is dedicated to our parents, Nelson and Artha Nassiff, for their love, literary advice, and encouragement throughout all of our endeavors and to Janice V. Adcock for assisting with the editing of the manuscript and for instilling a love of the past and its importance.

INTRODUCTION

The region, which contains the Adirondack Mountain range in New York State, has a long and intricate history. This rugged area, which has defied settlement by both Native Americans and Europeans, comprises approximately six million acres and contains over 2,000 high peaks, 2,300 lakes and ponds, and countless miles of rivers and streams.

Years before Europeans settled on the North American continent, Native Americans found comfort along the shores of Piseco Lake. Algonquins penetrated the mountains 12,000 years ago to hunt and fish during the summer months but were driven away by brutal winter weather. As Iroquois tribes traveled into the mountains from the south, they encountered resistance from the Algonquins. Mohawks and Algonquins fought many skirmishes over the mountainous region. The Mohawks, in contempt, called the Algonquins Hatirondacks or "tree eaters" because their diet consisted of tree buds and bark. Slightly changed, this word has identified the northern region of New York State as the Adirondacks since 1837. Many artifacts from the habitation of these early people have been found at various sites around Piseco Lake.

Samuel de Champlain was one of the first Europeans to gaze upon the Adirondack region. During his 1609 expedition to the New World, Champlain traveled down the St. Lawrence River and entered a large lake, which now bears his name. Looking west from these shores, Champlain surveyed rolling mountains and endless miles of forest land, known as the Great Wilderness by native dwellers.

There was very little European encroachment upon these lands until the late 1770s. During this time, the land encompassing Hamilton County was purchased from the Iroquois by Joseph Totten and Stephen Crossfield in 1771. These wealthy New Yorkers worked as agents for Edward and Ebenezer Jessup. The Jessup brothers lived in Albany and were engaged in land speculation and purchased over a million acres of wilderness land. In 1775, Totten and Crossfield applied for a patent from the British government to transfer the land titles. The American Revolution erupted suddenly in 1775, and land transactions were forgotten during the war between the American colonists and England. The Jessups organized the Kings Loyal Americans, a loyalist regiment that took part in the war. The brothers were captured during the Saratoga campaign and eventually were paroled and forced to flee to Canada. In 1785, Totten and Crossfield petitioned the state of New York for the original land claim. The state, in dire need of money, granted the title, and the land was divided into 50 townships. The area was now ready for sale and settlement as New York's expanding population moved across the state purchasing large tracts of land for speculation and agriculture.

Early American settlers were enticed by the abundance of affordable land and natural resources, and small communities were established throughout the area. The pace of settlement was slow in the rugged Adirondack Mountains. Roads leading north into the mountains were surveyed and cut. By 1810, a group of Shakers was clearing farmland on what became known as Arietta Road. By 1827, Seth Whetmore had founded the small community of Whetmore northeast of Piseco Lake. This settlement contained a sawmill and post office and led to the formation of a road from the town of Lake Pleasant. The road was eventually extended around the northern and western shores of Piseco Lake.

In 1834, Rensselaer van Rensselaer, a prominent citizen of Albany, began to purchase large areas of land south of Piseco Lake. Two years later, the New York State legislature divided the town of Lake Pleasant to form a new town named Arietta. Arietta Township was named after Rensselaer's mother and was populated by woodsmen, farmers, and lumbermen. By 1839, land developer Andrew K. Morehouse had founded Piseco Village and was establishing land contracts with new settlers at the head of Piseco Lake. Morehouse supervised the construction of sawmills to provide settlers with building materials. A year later, 15 families were living in the village. Morehouse's original plan called for five blocks of building lots, a courthouse, and six major streets to be named Hamilton, Washington, Jefferson, North, Center, and Court Streets. It is unknown to what extent Morehouse's elaborate plan was actually completed. By 1847, most of the settlers had become dissatisfied with harsh winters, short growing seasons, and Morehouse's strict contracts, and Piseco Village was nearly deserted. When the Civil War ended in 1865, the population of Arietta diminished to 82 residents.

Just as earlier settlers were leaving the area, the first tourists were traveling to Piseco Lake to fish in the unspoiled waters. Local residents saw an economic opportunity providing guide services and lodging for the new American sportsmen. In the late 1860s, the town of Arietta was revitalized by industry. The abundance of natural resources attracted entrepreneurs, especially in the lumber and tanning businesses. The greatly expanding country was in need of building materials, and lumber camps and sawmills could be found in different locations throughout the Adirondacks. Four sawmills were operating in Arietta, and large quantities of timber were floated down the Sacandaga River to mills in larger towns to the south. With a strong desire for leather in the shoe and glove industries in Johnstown and Gloversville, the need for tanneries near a hemlock tree source was essential. Two tanneries were operating in Arietta the latter part of the 19th century. Income was also generated by spruce gum picking, and transportation services needed to move the resources to market. The unrestricted use of natural resources in the Adirondacks brought much destruction to the environment, and many individuals feared for the future of the mountains. Land surveyor Verplanck Colvin prepared reports for the state legislature warning of these conditions in the wilderness. In 1885, the New York State legislature created the Adirondack Forest Preserve to protect the lands. In 1892, the Adirondack region was declared a state park.

Tanneries fell into decline in the late 1890s, and an influx of visitors initiated a boom in the tourist industry, bringing needed income to the local economy in the early 1900s. As transportation technology improved in the 1920s, a number of summer visitors erected permanent camps along the shores of Piseco Lake. With this new wave of tourists, employment opportunities improved, especially during the summer months. To handle this increase of visitors, local residents quickly furnished boardinghouses and hotels. However, making a living solely from summer tourists and fall hunters remained difficult. Many local entrepreneurs suffered financially in the off-season and during the Great Depression. Interest in winter sports during the post–World War II era and the commercial development of the snowmobile in 1955 have ensured the continued year-round success of the tourist industry in the town of Arietta. Through the years, Piseco has meant something special to the seasonal tourists and the people who have called Piseco their home. As quoted in *The History of Hamilton County* by Ted Aber and Stella King, Marion Banker, an early-20th-century tourist, expressed it best by saying, "My mother used to tell me that if I ever get to heaven . . . I wouldn't like it as well as Piseco."

One

CAST OF CHARACTERS

Every Adirondack community has an array of unique individuals who have defined their surroundings. The personal histories within the gathering of men shown are intriguing. Hobert Casler (far left) was arrested for shooting a local resident in a hunting incident. James Rourke (second from left) was wounded at the Battle of Bull Run during the Civil War. Richard Kempster (second from right) constructed a camp on Fall Stream. Peter Judway (far right) worked as a logger and merchant. These characters, among many others, have left their indelible mark by creating lasting memories helping to preserve the area's history.

Piseco Lake was named in the early 19th century by Joshua Brown, a surveyor from the town of Wells. Brown named the lake after Pezeeko, an old St. Regis Indian found living on the western shore of the lake. Piseco is an ancient Native American word derived from the word *pisco*, meaning "fish." The Native Americans therefore identified Piseco Lake as Fish Lake. (Illustration by Steven N. Nassiff.)

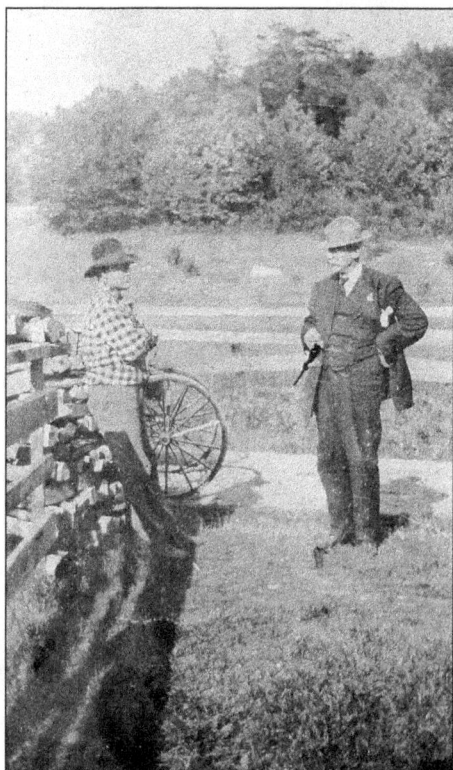

Born in 1855, Hugh Riley (left) is mainly known for the saloon he operated in Upper Rudeston during the 1890s. Riley was also a laborer and farmer and was still tilling the land at the age of 70. His wife, Agnes, operated the post office in the saloon from 1905 to 1907. Riley's house and saloon still stand today and are home to the Piseco Lake Historical Society.

The preservation of Piseco's historical heritage was initiated by real estate agent Gladys "Molly" Rockwell when she purchased the old Riley Tavern and homestead in 1954. In 1958, she offered the tavern to the Adirondack Museum, which rejected the donation due to financial restraints. Rockwell opened a small museum in the saloon to exhibit local artifacts. Not long after Rockwell's death in 1985, the Piseco Lake Historical Society was formed.

Shadrack Dunning, born in 1787, was the first permanent settler along Piseco Lake. His son Alvah Greene Dunning would become a legendary guide in the Adirondacks. By 1827, Shadrack was living near Piseco Lake and was a proficient hunter and trapper. Shadrack was well-known for his battles with Native Americans during his friendship with famous woodsman Nick Stoner. Shadrack died in 1830. (Illustration by Steven N. Nassiff.)

Famous Adirondack hunting guide Alvah Greene Dunning learned his woodcraft in Piseco and guided hunters in the Raquette Lake area. Sportsmen came from all points of the compass to meet this legendary guide. Successful Adirondack guides were multitalented individuals who provided a valuable service for visitors to the Adirondacks. While traveling in 1902, Alvah died of asphyxiation in a hotel in Utica. Alvah's knowledge of technological innovation must have been lacking; the gas lamp in his room had been leaking all night—he had blown out the flame. (Illustration by Steven N. Nassiff.)

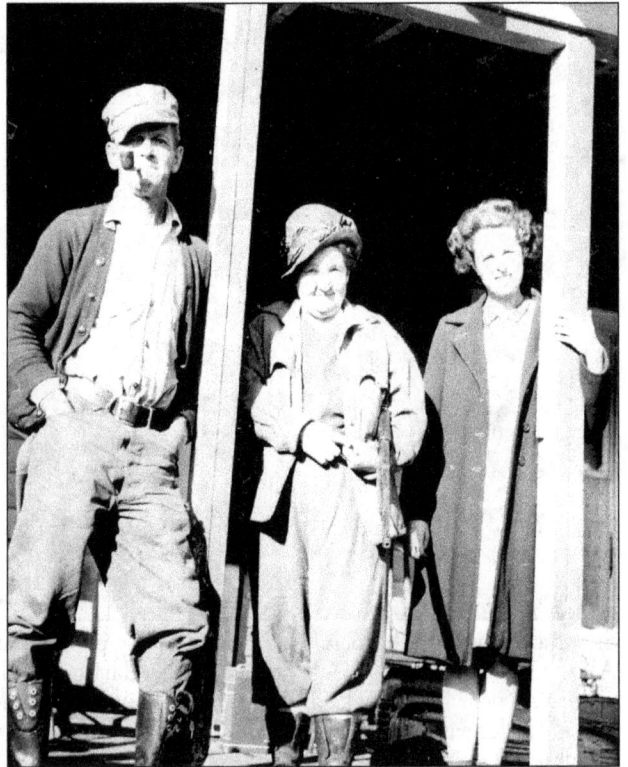

In 1896, Julia Ann Burton (center) was born to John and Annie Burton in a log cabin near Piseco Lake. At the age of 16, she married Charlie Preston (left) and two years later was guiding sportsmen for $10 a day toting her favorite Winchester rifle. Julia Preston was one of the first females to be licensed as a guide. Guides were known not only for their outdoor expertise, but for culinary skills, singing, and storytelling. In 1969, after 50 years of hunting, Julia Preston died at the age of 73. (Courtesy of the Preston family.)

Sanford E. Liddle came to Piseco as a sickly boy in 1912. His parents purchased a cottage near Fall Stream, and the outdoor life quickly restored his health. Liddle matured, along with the newly innovated airplane, and he developed a strong interest in flight. Liddle attended Parks Air College in St. Louis and was soon flying canvas biplanes in the skies over Piseco Lake, offering charter flights and transporting the U.S. mail. Liddle was a leading figure in establishing a permanent airport in Piseco.

Andrew K. Morehouse initiated much of the settlement of southern Hamilton County. By 1833, Morehouse purchased 15,000 acres of wilderness land and established a town, which to this day bears his name. He also oversaw the creation of a village at the head of Piseco Lake. Morehouse's unsuccessful attempt to persuade the state legislature to build railroads to his communities ensured the area's isolation. Morehouse died an inmate of the Oneida County Poor House in the early 1880s. (Illustration by Steven N. Nassiff.)

13

Floyd Ferris Lobb, or "Old Lobb," was born in Pennsylvania and traveled to Piseco in 1847. This cantankerous old fellow greeted strangers with the cry, "You had better go home—your mother needs you for soap grease!" Lobb's father, Isaac, came to Piseco in 1884 but drowned in the lake a short time later. After this tragic event, Lobb would never again fish on the Sabbath. Six years later, Lobb was found deathly ill by George Rudes and his sons. While rowing him back to Higgins Bay, a fishing line was placed in Lobb's hand, and his final request was fulfilled—he caught two trout. Lobb was buried in Higgins Bay Cemetery with a rod, reel, and several trolling spoons. A stretch of the western shore of Piseco Lake is still referred to as Lobbville. (Courtesy of the Blessing family.)

INVENTOR OF OLD LOBB TROUT SPOON
FLOYD FERRIS LOBB
1816 ——— 1891
AND HIS FAMILY.

Frank Rix, a summer resident of Piseco, was an avid photographer. Rix would quit his job in Ilion every summer and move to his cottage, Kamp Kodak, located on the west shore of Piseco Lake. Rix produced a number of photographic images of the area and was frequently seen moving his camera equipment by foot, boat, and bicycle. With his cousin William Billington he sold his postcards at local campsites for 5¢. Rix died in 1962, but his photographs preserve much of the visual history of Piseco Lake.

Leon (Len) Rupert Anibal, born in 1869, operated four hotels in Piseco as well as hotels in Speculator and Northville. Anibal retired from the business in 1946 when he sold his Anibal House hotel to George Haskell. His last enterprise was the operation of a small general store in Piseco Village, where at the age of 95, he was still naming his price for the merchandise.

David Brennan, or "Foxey Brown" as he was known in the Piseco area in the early 1900s, was a railroad worker who fled Boston believing he had killed a man during a fight. He settled into a lonely existence at his camp, Browns Ville, near Fall Stream, about six miles from Piseco Village. He was a cranky old fellow who would not permit strangers near his camp and would literally back up his words with buckshot. On November 10, 1916, Foxey Brown, Carleton Banker, and Frederick Bagg entered the woods to hunt. After the hunt, Brown could not locate Banker, and he and his companion ran to sound the alarm. The resulting five-day search was unsuccessful, and suspicion again fell on Brown. Unable to bear criminal allegations, Brown left the Piseco area. Six years later, William B. Abrams, a local guide, uncovered human bones while hiking in an area near the Spruce Lake trail. Rushing back to Piseco, Abrams notified the county coroner, and Carleton Banker's body was identified by the personal possessions found with the remains. Foxey Brown never returned to Piseco. (Courtesy of the Piseco Lake Historical Society.)

Ephraim Phillips, born in Amsterdam, New York, in 1802, served as sheriff of Hamilton County from 1843 to 1847. Phillips moved to Piseco and became manager of the Piseco Lake Hotel. He disappeared from the pages of history until 1890 when he wrote *Lucretia or Lost in the Adirondacks, a Tale of Love at Piseco*. This personal narrative, set in the environs of Piseco in 1861, recounts the tragic life of Orlando Howland and his family during the American Civil War.

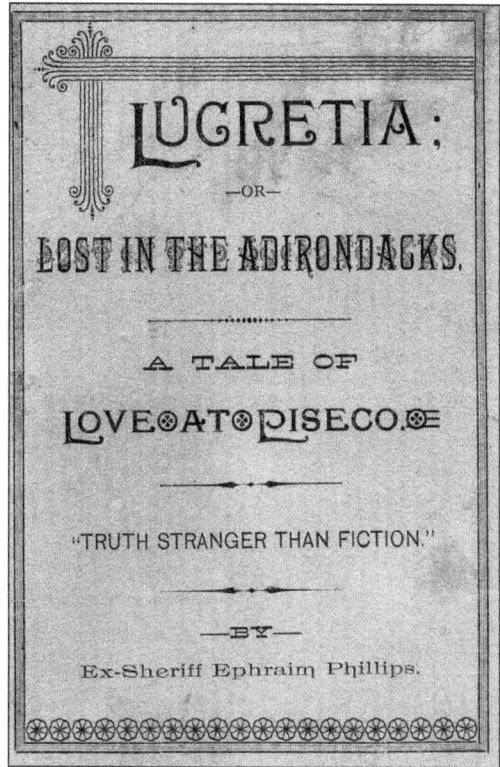

LUCRETIA;
—OR—

LOST IN THE ADIRONDACKS,

A TALE OF

LOVE ◉ AT ◉ PISECO. ◉

"TRUTH STRANGER THAN FICTION."

—BY—

Ex-Sheriff Ephraim Phillips.

The North American black bear is the main character in many Adirondack tales. Numerous stories center around the vicious battles hunters encountered when engaging a black bear. Black bears can weigh up to 700 pounds and are now the dominant animal in the Adirondacks, yet they were near extinction in the region by the early 1900s. For years, tourists flocked to the Piseco Lake dump to witness bears rummaging for food. Others have had chance encounters with these hungry intruders at their campsites.

17

Map of the Piseco Lake Area

The centers of population in the township of Arietta were mostly concentrated around Piseco Lake throughout the area's history. Small communities formed in Piseco Village, Upper Rudeston, Rudeston, and Lower Rudeston (or Higgins Bay) in the late 19th century. At this time, the permanent population of Piseco and the town of Arietta was approximately 400 inhabitants within its 2,100 square miles of wilderness.

Two

PISECO VILLAGE

After Andrew K. Morehouse established the town of Morehouse in 1835, he looked to the newly formed Arietta Township to create a model village and county seat. After purchasing a large amount of land, Morehouse initiated contracts with new settlers and sold building lots between Mill Stream and Cold Stream. By the early 1840s, several families were living in the village, which boasted a hotel, sawmill, and blacksmith shop, all with a beautiful view of the lake. Settlers soon became disenchanted, and by 1847, Piseco Village was nearly deserted. Over the years, the configuration of the village has evolved to meet the changing needs of the community.

This early view of a sparsely populated Piseco Village was taken in the 1880s. The residents of the village and visitors to the Piseco Lake Hotel (right center) had an unobstructed view of the lake during the 19th century. At this time, Upper Rudeston, with its thriving tannery, was the focal point of society in the Piseco area.

This view of Piseco Lake from Abrams Sportsman's Home is now completely obstructed by trees. Seen in the distance is the village school (note the outhouse), Irondequoit Club Inn, and Pine Island. This postcard, postmarked Piseco on July 29, 1909, was written by Lana Judway, wife of the Irondequoit Club Inn's manager, commenting that the inn has over 30 guests and the staff is very busy.

Individuals traveling from the west shore of the lake would have entered Piseco Village in this vicinity. At this time, the "bustling" village contained numerous homes, barns, and businesses, many of which are no longer standing. The rising ground near the pine tree hides the gurgling waters of Mill Stream.

Judway Brothers Grocery Store was located on State Road (now Old Piseco Road) running through Piseco Village. The store was operated by David and Peter Judway, who worked as loggers until establishing a grocery business. David served as postmaster from 1907 to 1912, and Peter managed the Irondequoit Club for 21 years. This structure is now a private residence.

This view of Piseco Village around 1921 shows Piseco Lake Hotel (large white building in middle distance), Cold Stream Bridge, Judway Brothers Grocery Store, the village blacksmith shop (first building on the left), and Lawrence's Ice Cream Stand. The site of the ice-cream stand is currently occupied by the Piseco Post Office.

The center of Piseco Village, as it appeared during the 1920s, shows the Piseco Lake Hotel (far right), which was used by various proprietors from 1849 to 1930. Across the dirt road is the Judway home with Judway Brothers Grocery Store in the background.

Piseco Tea Room, operated by the Dunham family, was located in Piseco Village and provided the community with a variety of services. In addition to serving lunches, dinners, and ice cream, the owners also provided patrons with groceries and gasoline. The Piseco Tea Room also served as the village post office during the years 1934 and 1935.

George Haskell and his wife, Helen, owned a general store and gas station on the main road in Piseco Village in the 1930s and 1940s. They also served as postmasters while operating the local post office from the store. This structure previously operated as the Piseco Tea Room.

Local female hunting guide Julia Burton Preston resided in a log cabin in Piseco Village in the 1940s, while her husband, Charlie, served in the military. In 1998, Julia's cabin, which still stands today, was marked with a New York State historical plaque.

Williams' Store was located in Piseco Village in the 1950s. This thriving business once stood across from the Piseco Airport but was demolished in the 1960s due to its unsafe location at the end of the airport's renovated runway.

Before 1840, the children living in what is now Arietta were educated in the town of Lake Pleasant. Mrs. C. E. Thompson was the teacher appointed at the first school built in Piseco Village, which was an uncommon occurrence since married women were rarely allowed to teach in public schools. Piseco Village schoolhouse, also known as District No. 4 School, was built on Haskell's Road in 1904. This school also served as the Sunday school, providing religious services to local children. Previous schools were instituted in lower Arietta, the Higgins Bay area, across from Oxbow Lake, and in Upper Rudeston near Silver Lake. By the 1930s, there was a need to transport students in the advanced grades to the school in Speculator and to the high school in Wells, several miles away. In 1949, the Arietta schools merged and land was purchased on Route 8 for the creation of the Piseco Elementary School, which is in use today.

This 1914 photograph shows the interior of the one-room schoolhouse in Piseco Village. At this time, the school was heated by a large central potbellied stove and was equipped with a pump organ. The annual operating budget for this school was approximately $700. In 1929, the school was updated to include a piano, a hot-air furnace, and two flush toilets that replaced the primitive outhouse. Piseco Village school operated until 1949 and is now in private ownership.

Len Anibal Trading Post was located in Piseco Village near the airport. Anibal operated the store into his 90s, selling a wide range of products, from fishing tackle to Woolrich outdoor clothing, making the trading post a unique shopping experience.

Three

AUTOMOBILES, PLANES, BOATS, AND TRAINS

By the 1860s, affluent people of the Northeast looked to escape the crowded cities and travel to the scenic Adirondacks. Despite emerging transportation technologies in the late 1900s, Piseco Lake remained an isolated area. Travel to Piseco took several days and required the use of steamboats, trains, and stagecoaches. With the advent of more reliable automobiles and better quality roads, vacation schedules changed. By the 1930s, many traveled to Piseco by motorcar for weekend visits to enjoy the Adirondack wilderness. Due to the abundance of waterways in the area, canoes, guide boats, and rowboats became a means of transportation and recreation.

Around 1900, tourists from the New York City area heading to Piseco Lake often began their travels at the Hudson River piers boarding a steamboat proceeding north to Albany. Facing this tiresome journey, vacationers packed steamer trunks preparing for long holidays in the mountains. The boat trip took most of the night, with the passengers waking at the state capital by morning. Travelers then boarded a train running on the Fonda-Johnstown-Gloversville Railroad and proceeded to Northville. A round-trip ticket from Albany to Northville cost $10.26.

Adirondack travelers arriving at the Northville train station would board stagecoaches to carry them into the rugged mountains. The first destination was the town of Wells located 15 miles to the north. Passengers had to endure the bone-jolting ride over rutted and dusty roads. At Wells, the travelers would rest as a fresh team of horses was hitched to the stagecoach to prepare for the journey to Piseco.

Stagecoaches were needed to carry travelers from railroad depots to Piseco Lake, since Hamilton County was considered one of the most remote locations in New York State in regard to train travel. In 1901, a stagecoach was robbed near North Creek, in which the bandits made off with $1,000, an interesting occurrence in the 20th century. This photograph shows Henry Courtney with his stage at Foote's Piseco Lake Inn located in Upper Rudeston near the Silver Lake Tannery. Foote's Inn burned in 1906 and was never rebuilt.

Guide boats were a preferred form of transportation on many Adirondack waterways. These wooden boats were favored by guides to carry sportsmen and provisions on hunting and fishing outings due to their stability in rough water and wind. Guide boats were designed to be lightweight and easily carried and could also be used as shelter. John F. Buyce, a blacksmith working in Speculator during the 1920s, was known in the region for producing these popular boats.

Original Native American canoe designs were sturdy and safe, even in rough waters, but with the addition of higher, comfortable seats introduced by Europeans, canoes became unstable. The popularity of recreational canoeing quickly spread through Europe and North America after John MacGregor, a Scottish lawyer, developed a practical canoe. Frank Rix photographed these women enjoying a canoe ride on Piseco Lake in the early 1900s. Despite their modest dress, women also participated in physical activities. Outdoor life quickly became synonymous with good health and adventure.

Canoeing on the crystal lakes scattered across this mountainous region has been a favorite pastime for generations of vacationers. Due to the formation of numerous canoe clubs during the 1870s, canoes were found in abundance on lakes and streams throughout the Northeast. This young lady tries her hand in a wooden canoe on the waters of Higgins Bay in the 1920s. The rowboat in the background mounts an early outboard motor.

The *Pocahontas*, built by the Toppan Boatbuilding Company, is a 24-foot gas-powered boat once used off the shores of Long Island. The boat, nicknamed the "Pokey," was transported to Piseco Lake in 1909 by Carl Schmidt to carry passengers and supplies to his camp at Point Comfort. Until the early 1950s, camps located in this area were accessible only by boat. The Pokey has been restored and can still be seen traversing Piseco Lake today.

C. E. Andelfinger owned a camp on the west shore of Piseco Lake. Since the road running along the west shore of the lake was generally in disrepair, Andelfinger purchased and operated a gas-launch boat named *Pastime* to transport people and provisions. This photograph shows *Pastime* docked at Point Comfort in the early 1920s.

Victorians could gaze across the wilderness lakes and see traditional canoes and guide boats rigged with mast and sail. Commercially made sailboats were later transported into the region, and small boat sailing became a recreation of great interest on Piseco Lake. Piseco Yacht Club was formed in 1959 to provide the sailor with an opportunity to compete with his fellow sportsmen. This photograph shows a trio of sailboats plying the waters of Higgins Bay as youngsters enjoy jumping from a homemade diving board.

In 1874, Christopher Columbus Smith created his first boat at the age of 13. Forty years later, the Chris Craft Company, based in Detroit, was widely known for producing quality wooden speedboats. Among Smith's customers were Henry Ford and William Randolph Hearst. William B. Abrams's Chris Craft is docked along the shores of Piseco Lake. Abrams, an amusement park owner, provided guide and taxi services as well as boating excursions on the lake for tourists. (Courtesy of the Abrams family.)

Automobile travel in the Adirondacks could be a harrowing experience. One-lane roads, thick mud, fallen trees, tire blowouts, overheated engines, and lack of gasoline stations made travel an adventure. Navigating single-lane dirt roads was equally difficult for horses and buggies. Prior to 1909, no roads in the Adirondacks were paved. The hazards of driving eased in 1916 when Arietta town supervisors began paving local roads with macadam (layers of compacted stone). William B. Abrams sits on the running board of his automobile surveying roadway conditions in Piseco. (Courtesy of the Abrams family.)

Tourism to the Piseco area was greatly increased with the emergence of the automobile. By 1914, American automobile assembly lines were beginning to flood the nation with affordable transportation. The availability of motorcars allowed people the freedom to explore and travel to remote locations, as evident by the string of cars in Piseco Village in front of the Anibal House in 1919.

This couple is seen touring the Adirondacks in style. A 1930 Cadillac LaSalle Roadster is parked along the shores of Piseco Lake at Higgins Bay. The couple, dressed for an outdoor adventure, is armed with a long-barrel turkey gun.

In the early 20th century, innovation met tradition as new automobiles started to share roads once reserved for horse and wagon. The convergence of transportation technologies was evident as the horse and buggy, automobile, and biplane could be seen simultaneously in Piseco Village. The horse barn still stands near the remains of the Lamkey Hotel, which burned down in 1930, as a Ford Model T sits idle across the road.

Before the automobile, horse buggies and bicycles were the major forms of transportation. The 1890s saw the golden age of the bicycle, as it provided recreation and a practical means of travel. As a result of this popularity, roadways were improved and women's fashions became less restrictive. This 1920s photograph shows Lena Judway at the Piseco Lake Hotel. Judway is pictured in her bloomers, which was considered controversial yet functional attire for bicycling at the time. (Courtesy of the Abrams family.)

The Adirondack region has an average seasonal snowfall in excess of 90 inches. The winter of 1915 saw one of the most severe storms to date in Hamilton County when a massive blizzard quickly dumped eight feet of snow on the area. Road clearance was virtually impossible, and many homesteads became dangerously isolated. A horse-drawn snowplow is shown clearing a road in the early 1900s. Wooden plows could cut a 14-foot-wide path through a moderate layer of freshly fallen snow.

Travel on rough Adirondack roads was difficult even in the best of weather. Spring rain turned dirt highways into impassable quagmires, and winter snows brought wheeled transportation to a complete stop. In 1901, the Arietta Town Board contracted to have two large snow rollers fabricated. These horse-drawn devices would simply compact the snow to allow the sleighs to pass. It took three days to clear the seven-mile stretch of road from Piseco Village down to the foot of the lake.

With the coming of winter snow, transportation methods in the Adirondack Mountains reverted to sleighs and heavy sleds drawn by horses or oxen. Snowplows and snow rollers prepared roadways by creating low-friction surfaces for vehicles with runners. This provided easy transportation of heavy loads not possible with a wagon. The lumber industry relied on huge sleds to remove logs from the forest. (Courtesy of the Abrams family.)

In 1925, Arietta, Lake Pleasant, Wells, and Hope jointly purchased a Holt rotary snowplow to maintain the road from Northville to Arietta. This slow-moving, gasoline-powered tractor was known for throwing snow a great distance during road-clearing operations. Local residents found other uses for this powerful vehicle as it was once used to move a sizable hotel in Speculator to a new foundation across the road. (Courtesy of the Abrams family.)

Float planes, or seaplanes, are a familiar sight in the skies over Piseco Lake. The abundance of lakes provide ideal landing sites for the bush pilots who fly this unique aircraft. Seaplanes aid in conservation efforts by stocking inaccessible Adirondack lakes with a variety of fish and are essential during fire patrols and rescue operations. Adventurous sportsmen chartered seaplanes to carry them to remote hunting and fishing grounds. (Courtesy of the Abrams family.)

William B. Abrams operated the first air service in the region from his waterfront campsite on Piseco Lake. Abrams provided charter flights for sightseers, photographers, and sportsmen. During the hunting season, seaplanes could be seen flying overhead with bucks lashed to the floats. Air services were also employed to fly building materials to remote locations during the construction of hunting camps. A crowd gathers on a beach to witness the flight of Abrams's biplane in the late 1920s.

By the 1920s, the popular trend of aviation had been introduced to area residents. An airfield was designated on the land of William Dunham in Piseco Village. Navigating Adirondack air currents was challenging, even for local flying enthusiast Sanford E. Liddle, who crashed two early biplanes at the airport. Canvas wing fabric and wires hung in the surrounding trees for many years. The town of Arietta purchased the property in 1960, and the airport is still in use today.

38

Four

EARLY HOTELS

By the late 1870s, Piseco Lake was a popular tourist destination. Sportsmen, campers, and vacationers enjoyed the fresh mountain air, cool lake waters, and beautiful mountain scenery. Over time, several hotels were established to provide hospitality to city dwellers, offering wonderful views of the surrounding mountains and pristine lakes. Visitors enjoyed a wide range of outdoor amusements such as deer hunting, trout fishing, mountain hiking, boating, and swimming. Haskell's Hotel, one of the many lodgings in the Piseco area, provided vacationers with food, drink, rest, and social entertainment from 1946 to 1978.

The old Piseco Lake Hotel may have been one of the original structures from Andrew K. Morehouse's unsuccessful attempt to create a village at the head of Piseco Lake. In 1876, William P. Courtney had taken management of the hotel from Ephraim Phillips and the Piseco Lake House became the social center of the area. This photograph shows Courtney's grandchildren on the front porch of the Piseco Lake Hotel in 1910.

Anibal House, formerly known as Piseco Lake Hotel, had been managed by a number of individuals throughout the years, including Len Anibal, who was proprietor of several hotels in the Piseco area. Sometime after 1910, a large addition was attached to the building and subsequent road grading changed the front porch elevation. The hotel was a popular tourist destination in the area from the 1850s to 1930s and had a picturesque view of the lake.

This image of the Anibal House in 1919 shows Cold Stream Bridge and the village blacksmith shop (far right). Vacation amusements were enjoyed in different forms, and on this day, William E. Lamkey's tamed black bear cub performs for guests at the hotel. Bear cubs were occasionally adopted by local hunters and guides after being separated from their mothers. Peddlers who sold essential wares to residents of isolated communities sometimes traveled with bear cubs to attract and entertain customers. (Courtesy of the Piseco Lake Historical Society.)

Since the first volunteer fire department in Piseco was not organized until 1947, fire was a constant threat of destruction to wood-framed buildings. The village hotel, known by various names in its 80-year history, burned to the ground in 1930 during its operation by William E. Lamkey. The bridge across Cold Stream can be seen in the distance, and the Judway house, shown across the road, still stands today.

OLD RUDES HOUSE.
Piseco Lake, Adirondack Mts.

In 1841, George Washington Bethune and a group of sportsmen from New York City and Troy formed the Piseco Lake Trout Club. During the club's nine-year existence, detailed records were kept of the amount of fish taken from the lake. By 1850, after having removed 6,356 pounds of trout, the club disbanded and sold the property to Eli Rudes, who opened the house to tourists. His son Daniel later took over, naming his inn Old Rudes Place. Daniel Rudes operated the hotel from 1857 to 1890.

Lamkey's Hotel, formerly known as Old Rudes Place, was operated by several proprietors over the years, including Fred J. Morey. Mary "Ma" Baker operated it as Piseco Tavern, and Rev. Andrew McAllister operated it as Bonnie Brae. Unlike lavish hotels in Blue Mountain Lake and Lake George, which catered to wealthy, distinguished travelers, accommodations offered at hotels in the Piseco area were simple, comfortable, and affordable. The rustic charm and seclusion found at Piseco Lake brought tourists back year after year.

C. Albert Doubleday of Montclair, New Jersey, had become captivated by the Piseco area during a hiking trip in 1877. He subsequently invited friends on return trips, and they formed the Piseco Company, which purchased land from the Adirondack Timber and Mineral Company. The acquired property contained a small farmhouse, and an additional structure was later moved to the site. The buildings became the Irondequoit Club Inn, incorporated in 1892.

This early-20th-century postcard shows the two main buildings of the Irondequoit Club Inn. The structure at left, called the annex, was moved to the site after the formation of the club in the 1890s. Unfortunately, the annex was dropped during the move, resulting in a permanent slant to the building. The structure on the right is an original farmhouse built in the 1850s.

The porches of the main lodge and annex at the Irondequoit Club saw countless gatherings as visitors bid farewell to their fellow tourists journeying back to the cities. Starr J. Murphy, seated in the back row, is seen with a group of vacationers in the late 1890s. Murphy, from Montclair, New Jersey, was one of the founding members of the Irondequoit Club with an original investment of $745.

This view of Piseco Lake, taken from the grounds of Irondequoit Club Inn, shows Mill Stream Outlet and Donohoes Point. In the middle distance is Pine Island, which had been purchased by the Irondequoit Club in 1917 for $750 with the stipulation that the new owners "shall quietly enjoy said premises."

A group of young women prepare for an Adirondack adventure at the Irondequoit Club Inn, complete with Native American garb, sidearms, and a pack basket. Pack baskets are one of the most recognizable outdoor accessories for Adirondack outings. These baskets, usually made of woven black ash splints with leather shoulder straps, were used to carry a variety of provisions and outdoor equipment.

The early-morning views of Piseco Lake from the porch of the Irondequoit Club Inn can be spectacular. The message on this 1947 postcard states, "Dear Grammie! Our vacation is almost over because the Club is getting filled up. But we still have time to swim, climb mountains and play Bridge."

Floyd W. Abrams, born in 1843, built the Sportsman's Home on Haskell's Road in 1880. Abrams offered visiting sportsmen guide services, accommodations, and the use of his hunting camp at T-Lake. Abrams and his wife, Mary, raised 10 children at this hotel. When tourism trends changed, the structure was converted into a private residence and eventually burned in 1956.(Courtesy of the Abrams family.)

In 1910, Truman Lawrence built a boardinghouse on what is now Haskell's Road. Like other Adirondack residents, Lawrence relied on various occupations to earn a living. He worked in the building trades, farmed land, and was town clerk in 1917. Sometime before 1915, he increased the size of his boardinghouse and renamed his hotel Lake View House. This 1915 postcard states, "Have been in the woods to work all winter, just got back home." The writer likely worked at a lumber camp in the Piseco area.

Before the innovation of electronic entertainment devices, people amused themselves in a variety of ways. The taming of wildlife was an interesting pastime exercised by some residents of the Adirondacks. Bear cubs, deer fawns, raccoons, chipmunks, and even certain species of birds were favorite animals to domesticate. In this photograph, a tame deer is being fed at Truman's Lake View House in the early 20th century.

In 1925, Leon R. Anibal purchased the Lake View House, renaming it Anibal House. The business was popular with summer tourists and fall hunters. George and Helen Haskell purchased the hotel from Anibal in 1946 and continued the tradition of fine food and generous hospitality. Haskell's Hotel was destroyed by fire in 1978.

Dining Room, Anibal House, Piseco, N. Y.

The dining room at the Anibal House was known for delicious fish dinners and meals of venison served family style. Under the ownership of George Haskell, a few old-time woodsmen earned their room and board by supplying the dining room with freshly caught whitefish and trout from Piseco Lake.

Anibal House. Lake Piseco n.y.

The front porch of the Anibal House shows evidence of a successful deer hunt during the 1940s. Proprietor Len Anibal can be seen standing at far right. Hotels in the Piseco area thrived during the hunting season by providing lodging, meals, and entertainment for visiting sportsmen.

Avery's hotel was built by Augustus Avery in the late 1800s as a travel stop between Lower Arietta and Piseco. Avery had purchased 1,000 acres of land along the West Branch of the Sacandaga River and in 1842 erected a log home and barn on this site. He raised six children in this isolated part of Arietta. Avery's Inn burned to the ground on April 24, 1926. At the time of the fire, the hotel was being operated by Augustus Avery's son Lyman.

Shortly after the destruction of his first hotel, Lyman Avery built a second structure with a two-story verandah, large dining room, and 100 guest rooms. This hotel was popular with hunters, lumberjacks, and road workers but was destroyed by fire in 1939. A few years later, Lyman Avery suffered the tragic loss of two sons who were killed during World War II.

Avery's Inn was known for the quality and quantity of its dinner menus as well as the panoramic view of the mountains from the front verandah. The dining room once served over 1,300 meals in one week and was the location for Saturday evening square dances.

In 1946, Robert Avery rebuilt a third hotel. This hotel served Adirondack tourists and sportsmen for over 50 years. Visitors remember the old-time atmosphere, hearty trout dinners, and the large, stuffed black bear that was displayed in the hotel's bar. This massive bear, which stood nearly eight feet tall and weighed 650 pounds, was shot by Robert Avery in December 1962. Avery's Inn closed in 1999.

This old waterwheel is located on the east side of Arietta Road just north of the former Avery's Inn. Lyman Avery installed the waterwheel to generate electricity for his hotel. Unfortunately, the 18-foot-diameter wheel would not produce the needed amperage for the electrical needs of the inn. Avery gave up on this innovative idea, and the ever-growing forest soon claimed the waterwheel.

Oxbow Inn, located on Oxbow Lake in Arietta, was originally operated as a boardinghouse by the Henry Rogers family. Religious services were held at the establishment prior to the formulation of a local Catholic church. The business expanded as the need to rent rooms and cabins to tourists and hunters increased. When the Tamarack Playhouse in Lake Pleasant was in operation, entertainers often boarded at the Oxbow Inn. Kirk Douglas was the most notable future celebrity to reside at the inn.

51

The town line separating Arietta from Lake Pleasant runs through Oxbow Lake. The land to the left is currently occupied by the Oxbow Lake Motel. In this area during the winter of 1862, the Isaac Monk family was trapped in their small home during a horrific blizzard. The family could not reach the woodpile to maintain a fire, and Monk's daughter died from the extreme cold. She was buried at her home near Oxbow Lake.

Piseco Lake Lodge, located at the foot of Irondequoit Bay, was built in 1920 as a private residence. In 1947, Royce and Marie Barnes purchased the property and opened a boardinghouse for the construction crews building Route 8. In 1960, public electricity finally reached the area and generators were no longer needed to power the lodge. Royce and Marie's daughter Jean and her husband, Chet Blessing, purchased the business in 1972, operating it for the next 27 years.

James Martin Rudes, a local farmer, operated an inn on the corner of Old Piseco Road and Lake Pleasant Road (Route 8). The inn contained a barroom that saw much activity during the height of the lumbering and tannery industries. Rudes, having raised eight children at the inn, farmed the land across the road (now occupied by the Piseco Elementary School). Rudes Inn burned down in 1918.

By 1925, Thomas Olmstead was operating a hotel on the previous site of Rudes Inn, located on the corner of Old Piseco Road and Lake Pleasant Road. This postcard, postmarked 1944, shows Olmstead's Hotel with its rustic furniture on the lawn and a deer carcass hanging from the front porch.

In the 1880s, a small settlement was formed near a thriving tannery in the southern part of the town of Arietta. The growth of this community was aided by the development of a sawmill, shingle mill, and large-scale lumbering operations. The area also contained numerous dwellings and two hotels. Patrick Tully operated the Arietta Hotel from 1887 to 1897. After Tully sold the business, a number of individuals managed the inn. The original hotel burned and was later rebuilt across the road.

GIRLS ARE ALRIGHT
In PISECO, N. Y.

Novelty postcards were designed to attract attention with their whimsical flavor. Postcards were sold in local hotel lobbies and stores and served as inexpensive souvenirs. A postcard and stamp could be purchased for 2¢, which was less expensive than mailing a letter. Before the widespread utilization of the telephone, postcards were used as a simple form of communication. This novelty postcard was mailed from Piseco Lake to May Whitman in Wells in 1913.

Five

GUIDES AND SPORTSMEN

The first sportsmen came to the Piseco area in the early 1840s. City dwellers traveled north to hunt and fish in the unspoiled wilderness and discovered an abundance of outdoor adventure. Piseco residents found employment guiding sports to wild game. Notable guides included Alvah Dunning, Floyd Lobb, Daniel Rudes, Tim Crowley, Floyd W. Abrams, and Julia Preston. Successful guides were multitalented individuals known not only for their outdoor expertise, but for culinary skills, singing, and storytelling. After 1895, year-round hunting and fishing was abolished when the Fisheries, Game and Forest Commission implemented game regulations, poaching laws, and separate hunting seasons.

The Piseco area was a well-known hunting ground for white-tail deer, black bear, wild turkey, grouse, and snowshoe hare. During the fall, Arietta Township was crowded with deer hunters. The humorous cry of "the red coats are coming!" was sounded among local residents as hunters in Woolrich red plaid field coats combed the woods. This group of sportsmen is gathered at Higgins Bay in 1931.

Ninteenth-century sportsmen were lured to Piseco Lake by huge schools of speckled brook trout, large quantities of whitefish, and the anticipation of battling a massive lake trout to the gunwales of the fishing boat. During this era, it was common for anglers to pull 20-pound lake trout from Piseco Lake. This fisherman has beached his boat and shows off his catch on the shores of Higgins Bay in the 1920s.

Various species of trout have been a favorite objective for fishermen on Piseco Lake for over 150 years. In 1852, Isaac Walton and a group of fishermen caught 483 pounds of trout in one week on Piseco Lake. The brook trout population was eradicated from the lake after a retaining wall burst on a private stock pond of pickerel on the Sacandaga River. As pickerel entered the lake, trout became their major food source, and brook trout soon disappeared from the lake. This trio of anglers trolls for fish near the west shore of Piseco Lake in the early 1900s.

Temporary dwellings, called shanties, were used to shelter sportsmen on their trips into the woods. Shanties were quickly assembled from available materials, such as wood and peeled bark. Local guide John Burton (far left) is shown at a bark shanty hunting camp at T-Lake in the early 1900s. Note the Winchester rifles, Adirondack pack baskets, and a barrel used as a chimney on the shanty.

Floyd W. Abrams, born in 1852, worked in the Piseco area as a logger, farmer, hotel proprietor, and sportsmen's guide. This photograph shows Abrams's hunting camp at T-Lake furnished with a large wood-burning stove. When asked how he was able to transport such a large stove into the backwoods, Abrams would state, "Well, I brought the stove in when he was a little guy and he just keeps growing and growing!"

Watercraft was essential to guides and sportsmen, even on small isolated lakes in the forests of Arietta. Transporting boats to these remote lakes was accomplished by horses, which could drag the boat along small wilderness paths for miles. This unique photograph shows a crudely made guide boat employed by two sportsmen returning to Floyd W. Abrams's T-Lake hunting camp after a successful hunt in the early 1900s. (Courtesy of the Abrams family.)

A group of woodsmen, equipped with pack baskets, fishing creels, and blanket rolls, is gathered at a log hunting camp near Piseco Lake in the early 1900s. Since shelter was essential for extended hunting and fishing trips in the woods, these primitive camps were furnished with such comforts as rustic tables and chairs, soft beds made of balsam branches, and the ever-present open fire used for warmth and cooking.

David Judway and his brother Peter came to Piseco in the 1880s to work in the logging industry. The Judways later boarded sportsmen at their log camp located at the foot of Irondequoit Bay. The single-lane road, or highway as it was once called, leads to Piseco Village six miles away. Note the logs in the lake destined for the sawmill.

David Judway's hunting camp in the year 1900 clearly illustrates the construction methods used to build log cabins. The building is assembled from logs placed horizontally and attached with a common joint. The space between the uneven logs is filled with a mud and moss mixture, called chinking, which helps seal the interior from weather and insects. Ceiling joists are notched into the log above the window to provide a second-story loft producing limited head space on the first floor. Similar to early American pioneers, Judway used hand-split cedar shingles as a roofing material. The photograph below shows the Judway camp years later in a dilapidated condition.

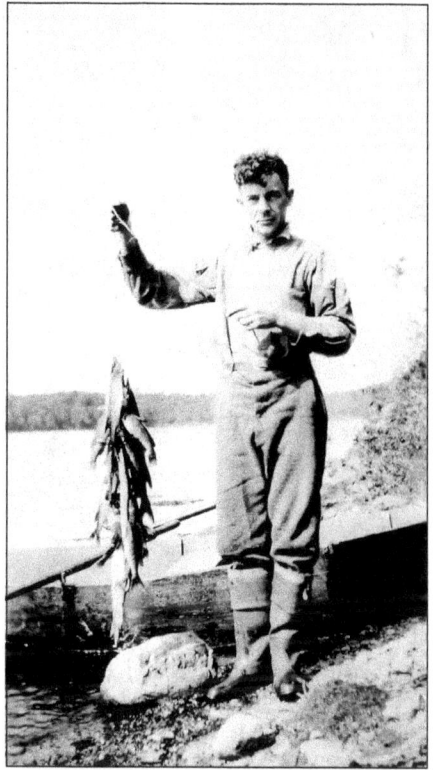

Good Luck Lake, located in Lower Arietta, has been a popular destination for hikers, woodsmen, and campers for over 100 years due to its sandy beach, shallow waters, and scenic beauty. The area around the lake has also been a focal point for industry. Henry Devereaux operated a lumber mill with a functional tram railroad extending a distance of 10 miles. In 1868, William Claflin established the Arietta Tannery at a nearby location. Good Luck Lake is named after an incident occurring in the early 19th century. During a surveying expedition, a musket was discharged at a cluster of water fowl and the barrel of the firearm exploded, sending pieces of metal in every direction. Luckily, no member of the party was injured, and the favorable outcome of this accident resulted in the name of the lake. As seen in these 1932 photographs, this fishing expedition at Good Luck Lake was very lucky.

A group of sportsmen at the Higgins home pose with lever-action rifles, a favorite sporting firearm in the late 19th and early 20th centuries since these guns were lightweight, reliable, and accurate. Repeating rifles allowed hunters to fire several rounds in quick succession without stopping to reload. The huntsman on the left carries his spare ammunition in a surplus U.S. Army cartridge belt.

An interior view of a camp in the Higgins Bay area, owned by George Chickering, is shown during the 1931 hunting season. In the fall, Adirondack hunters could encounter a wide array of weather conditions, ranging from warm autumn days to bitterly cold snowstorms. In typical Adirondack fashion, rustic chairs provide seating by the fireplace and wet wool socks hang over the cast-iron stove.

William B. Abrams, a local guide, leads a large hunting party at the Abrams camp at Vly Lake in the 1930s. Hunters have long been attracted to the North Woods due to the abundance of white-tailed deer. The Adirondack region was plainly identified on a 1761 English map as "Deer Hunting Country."

Trapping animals was an important source of income for farmers living in isolated Adirondack communities. During fall and early winter, trap lines were laid and monitored regularly. Beaver, muskrat, mink, rabbit, fox, and bear furs were greatly desired by the clothing industry. Trappers would trade or sell furs to local merchants who, in turn, sold them to furriers. Skilled trappers could earn $200 for their efforts during the winter season. The New York State Trappers Association was founded at Piseco Lake in 1953. A woodsman is shown with a large black bear taken in the Piseco area. (Courtesy of the Abrams family.)

Sportsmen from nearby cities often purchased small, inexpensive plots of land in the forest and created hunting and fishing camps for seasonal use. This uniquely civilized hunting camp located in the Piseco area is identified as "Never Inn." The wood-frame camp contains milled siding, glass windows, and lace curtains. Animal skins, rustic furniture, and a pack basket adorn the exterior of this Adirondack retreat.

Hunting techniques have changed drastically over the past 100 years in the Adirondacks. In the late 1800s, jacking, or hunting deer at night with a bright light, was legal. Guides also used dogs to chase down game for the benefit of sportsmen. After automobiles penetrated the forests in the early 1900s, there was a significant increase of hunters to the North Woods. This early photograph shows a hunting party, well clad in furs, transporting a buck in Arietta. (Courtesy of the Abrams family.)

Six

THE SHORES OF PISECO LAKE

Individuals traveling around Piseco Lake encounter towering mountains, rocky shores, sandy beaches, numerous camps, wildlife, and a variety of watercraft. Each unique feature on the lake holds special and enduring memories. For the past 100 years, Piseco Lake's 20-mile shoreline has provided visitors with rest and recreation away from the hectic pace of the busy world. Shown above is a group of businessmen from Poughkeepsie at the shore near Sunday Morning Camp at Higgins Bay preparing for a fishing expedition on the lake.

Pine Island & Mr. B. Abrams. Beach

Piseco Lake boasts a picturesque island that carries two different names, Pine Island and Club Island. This charming land mass rising from the lake has been exemplified by 19th-century writer Ephraim Phillips as "the peerless little isle that floats like a swan upon the bosom of Piseco." The name Pine Island was probably obtained from the number of large pine trees located on the island. This island is owned by the Irondequoit Club, hence it is also called Club Island. In 1942, workers at the Irondequoit Club were shocked to notice a fire burning out of control on the island. Armed with brooms and shovels, employees rushed to the island and fortunately brought the fire under control. Little damage occurred to the mighty pines that cover the island. This aerial view also shows Abrams Beach in the background (currently known as Half Moon Beach). (Courtesy of the Abrams family.)

Since the 19th century, Pine Island has been a popular destination for boaters. The north side of the island contains a small sandy beach and the interior is lined with foot trails. Picnickers would often hide coins around the island for children to discover on their adventures.

W. B. Abrams Field & Beach

William B. Abrams operated a waterfront campsite for approximately 20 years at the northeast end of Piseco Lake. The park included a carrousel (upper center), dance hall, large water slide, picnic grove, athletic field, and airfield. Visitors could also enjoy skeet shooting with .410 shotguns on a range near the carrousel. (Courtesy of the Abrams family.)

LAKE PISECO N.Y. From The North
Panther Mt. Pine Is. and Abrams Beach

Abrams Beach is arguably one of the best beaches in the Adirondacks. The golden sand gradually falls into the lake, and one can walk a lengthy 50 yards into the water on a velvety soft sandy bottom. The site was even popular to Native Americans visiting the area over 200 years ago. This stretch of shoreline is now referred to as Half Moon Beach and Golden Sands.

William B. Abrams originally flew a Travel Air seaplane that provided charter flights from his lakefront property. On a summer night in 1930, this aircraft mysteriously burned at Pine Island. Shortly after the loss, Abrams purchased WACO seaplane No. NC656N, built by the Weaver Aircraft Company of Troy, Ohio, in 1930. In this photograph, Abrams is operating a tractor at his seaplane hangar on Piseco Lake. (Courtesy of the Abrams family.)

68

In 1954, James and Barbara Ford, dairy farmers from Westtown, purchased a parcel of William Abrams's lakefront property and developed a seasonal campground. Sadly, the dance hall and carrousel had been previously removed. The Ford family operated Half Moon Beach for 51 years before selling the property to tenants.

In the early 1930s, the Corbett family from Binghamton purchased two vacant lots near the confluence of Oxbow Outlet and Piseco Lake. Near their waterfront camp, the Corbetts erected a replica of an ocean-side lighthouse complete with a revolving light and an attached boathouse. Local resident Floyd D. Abrams constructed the wooden structure, which stands approximately 25 feet tall. This unique landmark still overlooks Piseco Lake today.

CAMP GEHADA, LAKE PISECO, N. Y.

In the early 1920s, the sand beaches and rolling bluffs at the northeast end of Piseco Lake were occupied by the Herkimer County YMCA Camp and a Boy Scout camp named Camp Gehada. Camp Gehada provided recreation to visiting scouts and helped develop the boys' outdoor skills. A field kitchen is visible in the foreground as a group of boys play volleyball behind a row of tents.

The Herkimer County YMCA operated a summer camp, called Camp Piseco, in the 1920s. Postcards were sent soliciting funds to send boys and girls to camp in order to help develop their physical, mental, and moral qualities. Some 350 children attended Camp Piseco in 1922. In 1923, the YMCA sold a large portion of the land to private developers. These building lots were situated along a dirt path, which is now Pawling Road. Rudeston Mountain and Oxbow Mountain are visible in the background.

This unique postcard shows Higgins Bay and what is now known as Sherman's Point from the top of Pine Hill. Concealed among the trees is Charles R. Millham's rustic camp, and extending into the bay is Millham's dock and boathouse.

Higgins Bay has been a popular destination for tourists since the 1840s, when sportsmen first traveled to the area to fish in Piseco Lake. Before 1938, the village was known as Spy Lake and contained boardinghouses, a hotel, and a number of seasonal camps.

Throughout the early 1900s, three generations of Higgins men were active in the development of the area that bears their name, serving as guides, fire wardens, farmers, and business owners, as well as a school trustee, tax collector, and town supervisor. This photograph shows the Higgins homestead as it appeared in the early 1900s.

Pine Hill is a prominence overlooking Higgins Bay. When this photograph was taken in the early 20th century, the hill offered an unobstructed view of the area. Irondequoit Bay and Irondequoit Mountain are clearly seen in the middle distance. Higgins Bay Cemetery, where several local notables are buried, can be seen in the foreground.

In 1884, Dr. Edward L. Trudeau introduced the first tuberculosis sanitarium near Saranac Lake. Soon after, hundreds of tuberculosis patients flocked to the Adirondacks to seek treatment and rest in the clean mountain air and healthy climate. A small tuberculosis sanitarium was operated by Dr. Hackert near the shores of Higgins Bay in the early 1900s. Local residents supplied the sanitarium with garden produce, fish, and game. The facility was sold in 1918 and was converted to a seasonal cottage still in use today. (Courtesy of the Ackerman family.)

This 1930s photograph shows the East Piseco Store in Spy Lake operated by James E. Higgins. This general store offered a variety of goods, including gasoline. Ebba Higgins ran the post office from this location from 1938 to 1962.

This 1914 postcard shows Higgins Bay looking northeast. One hundred years ago, much of this area was used as farmland and pasture. The split-rail fence, shown in the center of the photograph, extends into the lake—a sure way to keep livestock from wandering.

In 1900, American industrialist George Eastman introduced the first mass-produced consumer camera, named the Kodak Brownie. Armed with cameras, tourists produced tens of thousands of photographic images of the Adirondack wilderness over the years. This photograph, produced by a Brownie camera, shows a tourist sitting along the shores of Piseco Lake in 1929. Piseco Mountain dominates the background.

74

As part of Pres. Franklin Roosevelt's New Deal policy, the Works Progress Administration (WPA) was created. This program employed millions of Americans to build public structures and roads. Southwest of Higgins Bay, a WPA project was initiated in the 1930s to construct South Shore Road. Art Shelmandine of Amsterdam, New York, was the first individual to purchase a building lot from the International Paper Company in this area.

Many camps along the shores of Piseco Lake were personalized with a name chosen by the owner. Often these names were derived from the Native American language or from natural features located near the property. Over time, camp names customarily remained the same, even with a transfer of ownership. Camp Blue Water, located in the Higgins Bay area, is shown in this 1940s photograph.

75

South of Higgins Bay is a small inlet called Benton's Cove, named for Tyler Benton, who lived in the area in the 1820s. Benton's Cove was identified in Sheriff Ephraim Phillip's 1890 book *Lucretia*, where the recluse Howland family was located by a local search party in 1861. Throughout the years, this area of water has also been identified as Benton's Gulf or Benton's Gulph.

A view of the south end of Piseco Lake shows Irondequoit Bay and Old Piseco Road in the early 1920s. This would have been the first glimpse of the lake for people traveling to Piseco Village on Hoffmeister Road. Point Comfort can be seen in the middle distance.

Panther Mountain has been a popular hiking destination for over 150 years. A three-quarter-mile trail leads up to Echo Cliffs, which crown a 700-foot precipice. These cliffs offer spectacular views of the lake and surrounding countryside. Many outdoorsmen cherish the magnificent sight of the sun rising while perched on the edge of Panther Mountain.

Piseco and Spy Lakes from Little Panther Mt.

Literally thousands of photographs have been taken of this view from the top of Panther Mountain. Piseco Lake is shown in the foreground, Spy Lake in the distance, and Higgins Bay at upper left. The name Panther Mountain stems from the abundance of panthers that populated the area in the early 1800s. In 1837, the Arietta town board placed a $20 bounty on panthers to rid the area of this predator.

Irondequoit Bay and Piseco Outlet can easily be seen from the top of Panther Mountain. The sliver of water, shown in the distant left, is Big Bay. Also pictured is a view of Point Comfort at the opening of Irondequoit Bay, where several large rustic camps were built in the early 20th century. Note the vintage graffiti on the rocks in the foreground.

In 1920, the New York State Conservation Department began developing 15 public campsites in Hamilton County, three being located on Piseco Lake. The campsites were named Poplar Point, Little Sand Point, and Point Comfort. Point Comfort Campsite opened to the public in 1931. The naming of this campground was a source of displeasure to summer residents whose land across the bay was already identified as Point Comfort.

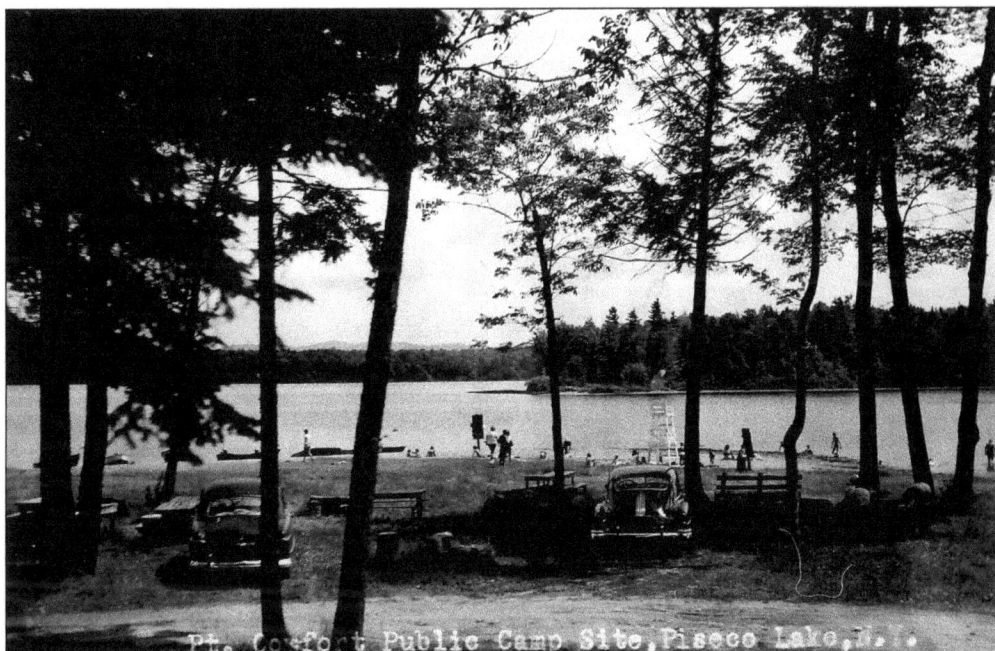

Pt. Comfort Public Camp Site, Piseco Lake, N.Y.

The dangers of the wilderness were evident in 1943 when a double drowning occurred at Point Comfort Public Campsite. Local residents attempted an unsuccessful rescue, and one of the bodies was recovered with the use of a fishing rod and hook. By the 1950s, state campgrounds began adding amenities such as life guard towers to increase the safety and enjoyment of their campers.

PISECO N.Y. 1931

"How much closer can we get before we get into trouble?" This view of the west shore of Piseco Lake in 1931 was taken from what is now Little Sand Point campground. The lake level was naturally low prior to the construction of a dam at Piseco Outlet in the 1950s. Note the lifesaving apparatus hanging on the post under the tree.

79

Sunbathers enjoy the warm sands and refreshing waters of Piseco Lake at Little Sand Point in the 1950s. The campground was opened to the public in 1953. In the background, Piseco Mountain towers above the lake waters.

Located on the west shore, Big Sand Point, a sand embankment jutting far into Piseco Lake, was a popular gathering spot for swimming and boating outings. Over the years, thick lake ice began to erode the prominence. After a dam was installed in the 1950s to control the water level in Piseco Lake, this area became submerged.

Big Sand Point was once a favorite bathing area for summer tourists. In the early 1900s, bathing suits for men and women were customarily made of wool and extended to the knees to offer a modest appearance in public. Women usually sported bathing caps and stockings to complement their loose-fitting suits, enabling them to participate in water sports. Women ordinarily preferred wading to swimming, since woolen bathing suits could be heavy and restrictive when wet. Early swimsuits for men and boys consisted of one piece, formfitting garments, usually with long sleeves and legs. At this time, many individuals were very cautious in the water, since opportunities to develop strong swimming skills were limited. Waterways around larger cities could be polluted and unhealthy, which made swimming in the Adirondack waters an enjoyable experience for visitors.

Fannie Brayton owned this cottage, located in front of Big Sand Point, in the early part of the 20th century. By 1925, the number of summer residents at Piseco had greatly increased since new and improved roads and the availability of automobiles brought more visitors to the area. The development of summer cottages provided various employment opportunities for local residents.

These seasonal camps were located along the west shore of Piseco Lake. Due to current environmental regulations, camps can no longer be placed near the water's edge. This vintage postcard states, "We are still in this delightful spot and probably will be for another month." Vacations to the isolated mountains could be very lengthy for travelers in the early 20th century.

A view along the west shore of Piseco Lake in the early 1930s shows *Pastime*, a wooden boat owned by C. E. Andelfinger, docked in front of a seasonal camp. *Pastime*'s canvas canopy provided shade for the passengers as they cruised the lake, since exposure to the sun was not desirable at the time. A combustion-engine boat was a rare sight on the lake and routinely drew curious spectators to the shoreline.

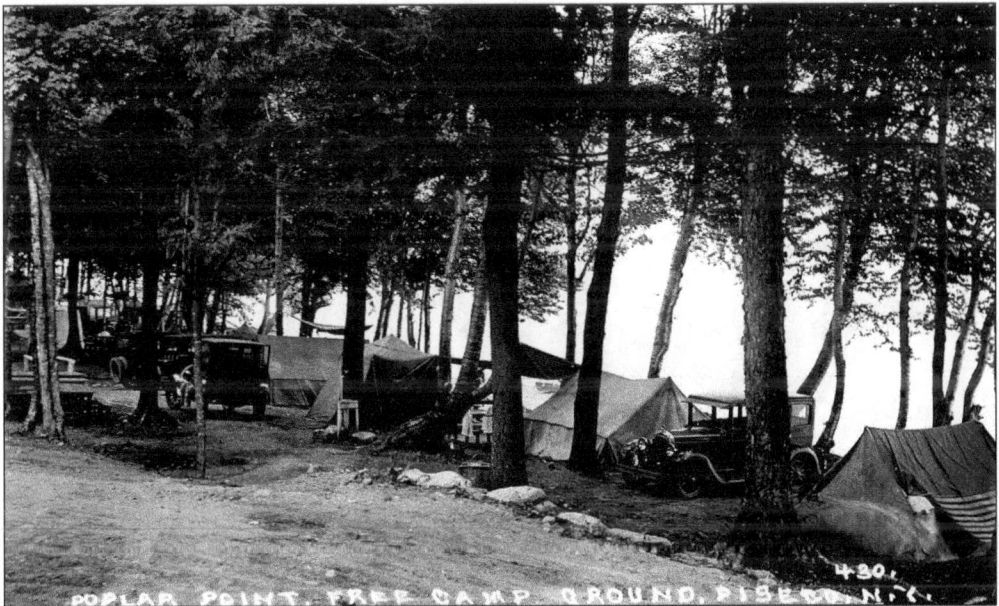

The popularity of tent camping is evident at Poplar Point Campground, as it appeared in the 1930s. Affordable canvas tents made it possible for countless families to enjoy the natural settings of the Adirondacks. State campgrounds in the area were often constructed with the assistance of the Civilian Conservation Corps (CCC), which was a national employment program initiated during the Depression years of the 1930s. Poplar Point Public Campground opened in 1927.

Pine Island, Rudeston Mountain, and Oxbow Mountain can clearly be seen in this photograph taken from the top of Piseco Mountain in the early 20th century. At this time, the hike to the summit of Piseco Mountain, with an elevation of 2,729 feet, was a popular outing for visitors to the Piseco area.

This visitor to the Irondequoit Club Inn poses on top of a large piece of driftwood on the shores of Piseco Lake in the late 1890s. At this time, city dwellers were generally fascinated with the extraordinary natural elements not seen in their everyday life. Pine Island can be seen in the background.

Seven

CAMPS

In the Adirondacks, any cottage, cabin, trailer, or tent is referred to as a camp. In the early 1900s, individuals purchased land and constructed lodgings for weekend use, extended vacations, and sporting excursions. These structures ranged from canvas tents and crude shanties to large buildings designed by architects, carefully assembled by local craftsmen using natural materials found in the forest. Today some of these early camps can still be found in the forest and along the shores of Piseco Lake, each with a unique history and enjoyed by succeeding generations of original owners.

Tent camping became very popular following the Civil War. By the 1870s, hundreds of canvas tents dotted the shores of Adirondack lakes. This photograph taken by Piseco summer resident Frank Rix shows an elaborate Adirondack campsite. Note the carpet on the tent floor, an oil lamp, hanging artwork, a fabric hammock, interior wall tapestry, and evergreen decorations throughout.

In 1882, the Potter brothers raised the first wood-framed camp along the west shore of Piseco Lake near Floyd Ferris Lobb's isolated shanty. Four years later, Dr. Will Tremain of Rome, New York, purchased the camp and became the first permanent summer resident on Piseco Lake. Dr. Tremain became friends with "Old Lobb," visiting him regularly to hear his interesting tales of hunting and fishing in the surrounding wilds.

The Adirondack region is known for its unique, rustic architectural style. This multiple-story camp on the shores of Piseco Lake exhibits natural features with its use of logs and decorative wood accents. The message on the back of this 1908 postcard states that Prince, the St. Bernard dog shown in the picture, "greatly enjoys swimming in Piseco Lake."

Campers prepare for a Fourth of July celebration on Piseco Lake in the early 1900s. This flag-draped camp was located along an area on the western shore of the lake known as Lobbville. This area was named after Floyd Ferris Lobb, one of the first residents who settled along the west shore of Piseco Lake.

Piseco Lake tourist Richard C. Kempster raised a permanent residence along Fall Stream in 1900. This photograph shows the house during the final phases of construction with a total building cost of $900. Currently the building is a private residence.

In 1900, Carl Schmidt purchased two lots of land at the foot of Piseco Lake from the International Paper Company. Schmidt, a musician and teacher from Brooklyn, built a camp on this site in 1903. This rustic structure, with a panoramic view of Piseco Lake, was named Point Comfort and has remained in the family for over 100 years.

SCHMIDT'S CAMP-POINT COMFORT-PISECO LAKE, ADIRONDACK MTS.

In the 1920s, the Schmidt family attached an addition to the original camp. This extension, which ran off the camp at a slight angle, contained additional bedrooms and a unique storage room covered with tin plate. All textiles and mattresses were stored in the tin-lined room to protect them from woodland rodents. Carl Schmidt's musical talents prompted summer evening concerts and sing-alongs on this stretch of shoreline.

In 1904, Frank Jennings had a rustic retreat constructed named Camp Irondequoit. At the time it was built, the area was accessible only by boat and supplies needed to be ferried across Irondequoit Bay. Much of the building material was acquired from the surrounding forest. This structure exhibits unique Adirondack architectural features, including a large central stone fireplace, wraparound verandah, applied bark, and timber siding. Currently Camp Irondequoit is privately owned.

The elaborate interior of Camp Irondequoit matched its rustic exterior. The use of logs for decorative fretwork is clearly seen in the camp's great room. A large root table, hunting trophies, firearms, fishing creels, and snowshoes complete the Adirondack decor. The camp also featured an assortment of handmade rustic furniture. A tin room kept linens, blankets, and clothing safe from mice in the off-season.

The opposite side of the great room at Camp Irondequoit is centered around a large stone fireplace adorned with a moose head and Native American pottery. An array of international flags hangs from the roof rafters above the bark-covered door. The large and decoratively carved tree fungus on the stone mantle is an example of a unique craft enjoyed by visitors to the Adirondacks as a personalized souvenir.

Native materials were used in the development of Camp Irondequoit and created a rustic look often desired by Adirondack camp owners. The screened porch is a necessary defense against mosquitoes and black flies in the Adirondack region. The birch rocking chair seen on the porch may have been produced by Lee Fountain of Wells, who specialized in building this type of chair.

Camp Irondequoit was built for the Jennings family with the help of William Lamkey Sr., who is pictured on the front porch with a large collection of hunting trophies. Lamkey, a well-known citizen of the Piseco area, was a veteran of World War I who served as a sergeant in the 303rd Infantry Regiment in France.

View from Point Comfort, Piseco Lake, N.Y.

The camps located on Point Comfort have an unobstructed view of Piseco Lake and the surrounding mountains. The wooden watercraft docked along the shore were used for recreational purposes as well as traveling to Piseco Village in search of supplies since it was more favorable to row six miles on the lake than to travel on the rough roads to the village.

In 1919, Luther and Nellie Holmes purchased land along Irondequoit Bay. Nellie's brother, architect Albert E. Price, designed this immense rustic camp built in 1924, naming it Onetah Lodge. Workers, materials, and furnishings, including a concert grand piano, needed to be transported to the site by boat. Not all of the Holmes family belongings made it across Piseco Lake safely, and it is believed a cast-iron stove rests at the bottom of the lake today.

The design of the Holmes camp combines a variety of Adirondack architectural features commonly found in the early 1900s. Many of these characteristics had been augmented by famous land developer and amateur architect William West Durant in the late 1800s at Camp Pine Knot on Raquette Lake. Embellishing the design of the traditional American log cabin and incorporating elements of Swiss and Japanese architectural accents, Durant developed a unique form of structural design commonly referred to as Great Camp architecture. Architect Albert E. Price used these same principals when he designed the Luther Holmes camp in the early 1920s. The camp contained a large verandah, icehouse, water tower, and great room with a large stone fireplace. The great room was surrounded by an interior balcony offering access to a series of bedrooms.

Charles R. Millham built a summer home on Piseco Lake in the early 1900s. This impressive log structure contained several features seen in the newly-developed prairie architecture style. Note the broad, gently sloping roofs and long verandahs creating large outdoor living spaces.

The interior of the Millham's camp in Higgins Bay contained a spacious living area surrounding a large stone fireplace adorned with a moose head. The Adirondack camp offered upper-class citizens a haven not only from the hectic city life, but an escape from the ills of society. Diseases, such as tuberculosis and polio, and social unrest compelled many leading citizens to temporarily evacuate their urban surroundings for the solitude of the mountains.

94

In 1924, the Knox family, founder of the famed Knox Gelatin Company of Johnstown, built a large camp and massive boathouse on the northeast side of Piseco Lake. In 1944, the family also raised an airplane hangar to house a biplane, which could be seen flying regularly over the lake. The camp and outbuildings continue to be used today by members of the Knox family.

In the past, boathouses were a common sight on Adirondack lakes. These waterfront structures were used to store and protect wooden boats. Watercraft, ranging from canoes to large speedboats, could be directly steered into the boathouse. Upper levels were used as retreats, studios, or servants quarters. With the coming of cold weather, many boathouses would be disassembled and moved to firm ground to avoid destruction by winter ice. The Knox camp contains one of the few remaining permanent boathouses on Piseco Lake.

This rustic camp, owned by the Benson family, overlooks Higgins Bay and was built in the late 1800s. For several decades, modern conveniences such as indoor plumbing, electricity, and central heating were not available. Camps relied on fireplaces and stoves, outhouses, and water wells to meet their essential needs. By 1933, the New York State Power and Light Corporation had extended electrical power to the Higgins Bay area.

In the late 1800s, a number of camps using wood-frame construction techniques appeared along Piseco Lake. This building process used factory-cut lumber and nails to quickly and economically assemble the frame, roof trusses, and exterior sheathing. A group of well-dressed visitors enjoy the fresh mountain air at their seasonal camp on the shores of Piseco Lake in 1907.

This Frank Rix postcard shows the interior of a camp located at Piseco Lake. As with other Adirondack camps of the time, the rustic decor included a stone fireplace, firearms, and framed woodland scenes. The door to the right of the fireplace is accented with a number of carefully arranged tree fungi. This postcard was mailed on August 9, 1909, to Charles Rix of Ilion, brother of photographer Frank Rix.

Chanopa Lodge, or the Price camp, is situated along the shores of Irondequoit Bay. The camp was designed and built by Cornell graduate Albert E. Price, an architect who worked for the Texas Company (Texaco). The stone structure was built using locally-acquired materials, and the framing timbers were obtained from the covered bridge in Wells when it was dismantled in 1929. The camp was in an ongoing state of construction from 1926 to 1950 and continues to serve as a retreat for the Price family. (Courtesy of the Price family.)

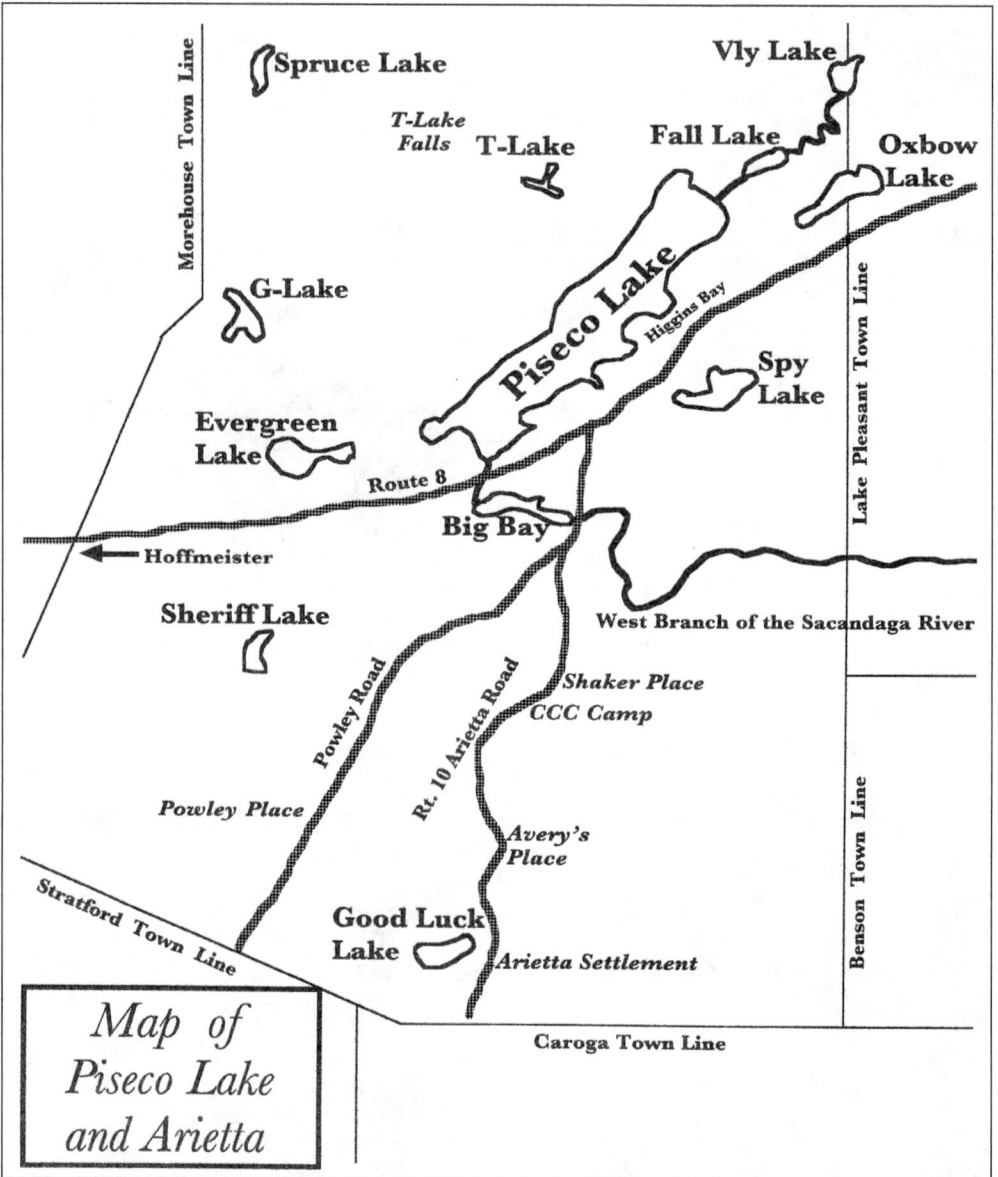

Map of Piseco Lake and Arietta

Spruce Lake

Vly Lake

T-Lake Falls

T-Lake

Fall Lake

Oxbow Lake

G-Lake

Piseco Lake

Higgins Bay

Spy Lake

Evergreen Lake

Route 8

Big Bay

Hoffmeister

West Branch of the Sacandaga River

Sheriff Lake

Powley Road

Rt. 10 Arietta Road

Shaker Place

CCC Camp

Powley Place

Avery's Place

Good Luck Lake

Arietta Settlement

Stratford Town Line

Caroga Town Line

Morehouse Town Line

Lake Pleasant Town Line

Benson Town Line

The township of Arietta is approximately 30 miles wide and 70 miles long with Piseco Lake as the dominant geographic feature. Railroad companies saw little need to lay tracks to the Piseco area, which has ensured its relative isolation to this day. Early visitors were forced to endure long, uncomfortable journeys on Arietta Road, Hoffmeister Road, and the road running from Lake Pleasant. All roads leading to Piseco remained primitive well into the 20th century.

Eight

THE SURROUNDING COUNTRYSIDE

The diversity of features in Arietta has long been an attraction for travelers wishing to experience the appeal of nature. Most of Arietta's 2,100 square miles is wilderness and contains curiosities that have fascinated visitors throughout history. The region possesses historic remnants, including industrial ruins, one-room schoolhouses, the CCC camp, YMCA and scout camps, and unique forms of architecture. Natural features such as waterfalls, wildlife, mountains, lakes, and vestiges of old growth forest have lured generations of settlers, entrepreneurs, and tourists. Pictured above is T-Lake, a popular destination for sportsmen for over 100 years.

The earliest settlers in Arietta were a group of Shakers from the religious settlement near Albany. The Shakers raised a series of buildings and cleared the surrounding forest for crops. They manufactured a variety of wood products, including bakers' peels, which were used to remove bread from large ovens. By 1820, the Shakers abandoned the site and Eli Rudes took up residence at what would be known as Shaker Place.

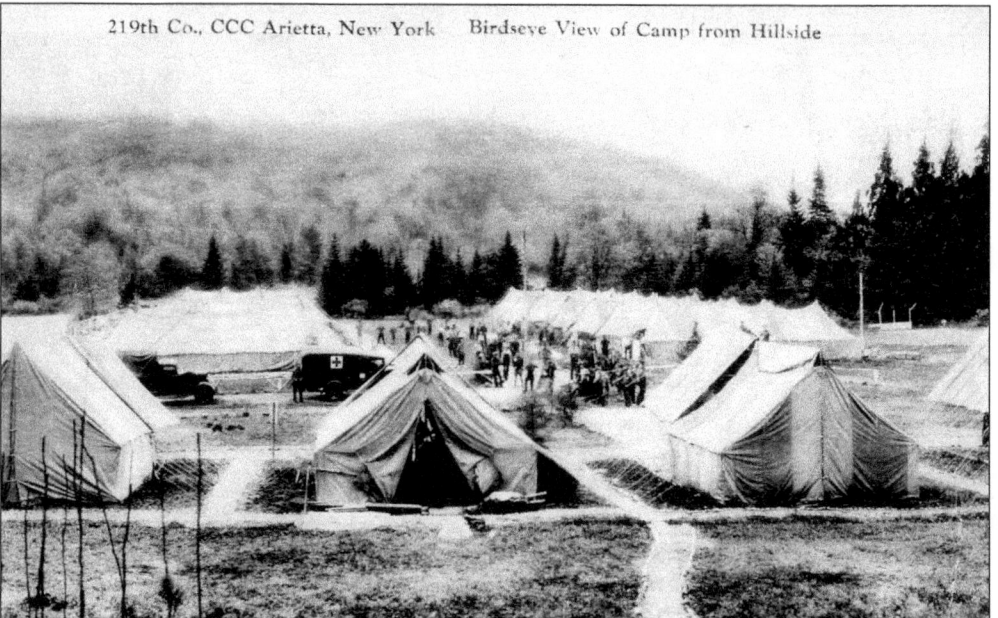

219th Co., CCC Arietta, New York   Birdseye View of Camp from Hillside

Following the 1929 stock market crash, Pres. Franklin D. Roosevelt organized the CCC to employ young men. The first CCC Camp in New York was located in Arietta at the old Shaker Place. The 219th Company, stationed at this camp in 1933, carried out projects such as tree planting and road work. CCC members made $30 a month to help support their families. A state historical marker identifies this site on Route 10.

In 1880, German immigrant John Powley moved to Arietta and built a farm on Piseco-Stratford Road. By 1892, Powley found farming the rocky soil was best left to others, so he abandoned the land. During the early 1900s, the property, called Powley Place, was being used as a boardinghouse for visiting sportsmen. The name of the boardinghouse was changed temporarily in 1915 to Pauley Place by proprietor Henry Radley. Today this area bears the original name of the Prussian farmer who first settled the land.

Spy Lake, south of Piseco Lake, was named in 1810 by a surveying party led by famous woodsman Nick Stoner when the group suddenly stumbled upon this hidden body of water. Stoner, a legendary folk hero in Fulton County, served in the Continental army during the American Revolution. This famous trapper, woodsman, and veteran died in 1853 at the age of 91.

Sheriff Lake is located southwest of Piseco Lake and was originally owned by Colt Firearms Company. The Colt company called the property Kego Park and used it as a private retreat for executives and customers. Colt sold the property in 1930. This photograph shows the woodland trail leading to Sheriff Lake.

West of Piseco Lake near the Morehouse town line sits G-Lake. The name of the lake has been derived from the peculiar shape of its shoreline. The camps in this area eventually became state land and were burned to the ground in the 1970s as part of New York State's Adirondack Park Agency Act, which attempted to revert land back to its original natural state. This photograph shows the Salamon family cottage at G-Lake as it appeared in 1915.

Municipal garbage collection is a recent public service. In years past, rural families disposed of waste in private dumps. Even today hikers of the Adirondack woods frequently stumble upon old debris piles, which provide some insight into the lives of previous generations. A garbage dump at G-Lake, used in past years by local campgrounds, is visited by a black bear in search of food scraps—a common occurrence before the recent mandate to remove all refuse from the Adirondack Park.

After a devastating 1903 forest fire, 600,000 acres of timberland were destroyed in the Adirondacks. State legislation was soon passed for fire detection and prevention. By 1918, fifty-two fire towers had been erected in the region. While building the T-Lake Mountain fire tower near Piseco, during a severe thunderstorm, a lightning bolt struck a tent, rendering all five workers unconscious. Fortunately, all of the men fully recovered.

This photograph shows the fire ranger camp at the T-Lake fire tower. The camp was a popular stopping point for hikers on their journey to T-Lake Falls. The fire tower and ranger camp were destroyed in the late 1970s along with other towers in the Adirondacks after state officials bowed to the demands of environmental groups. (Courtesy of the Abrams family.)

T-Lake Falls is located west of Piseco Lake and drops over 600 feet. It was a popular hiking destination for several years until New York State closed the dangerous overlook due to the number of injuries and fatalities incurred by visitors.

To properly appreciate the size and beauty of T-Lake Falls, visitors must descend by rope to the rocky bottom of the massive cascade. Pictured is a young female hiker climbing down a cable at T-Lake Falls in 1949.

View of Metcalf Mountain from top of T Lake Falls, Adirondack Mts.

The top of T-Lake Falls offers spectacular views of Metcalf Mountain and the surrounding countryside. This postcard's message, written by Annie Liddle, describes a hike to T-Lake Falls led by local guide George Abrams. Annie was the wife of Dr. Henry Liddle, an esteemed physician in the Piseco area during the early 1900s, who routinely provided his medical services free of charge.

Northeast of Piseco Lake is a small body of water named Vly Lake, which is accessible from Piseco by canoeing five miles up Fall Stream and Fall Lake. This postcard shows a canoeist visiting William Abrams's hunting camp at Vly Lake in the late 1920s.

Fall Stream is one of the larger tributaries flowing into Piseco Lake. Local hermit Foxey Brown lived on the banks of the meandering water during the early 1900s. For years, the stream was a favorite spot for anglers. In the 1930s, local children Bill Abrams and the Courtney brothers snagged a vintage high-wheel bicycle from the pool at Fall Stream that had been stolen years before. Fall Stream is now a popular canoe route leading to Vly Lake.

This 1906 photograph shows the steel bridge over Fall Stream located on Old Piseco Road. The iron bridge, originally built in 1900, was replaced by a concrete bridge in the 1930s. Anglers from points as far as Utica would make the 50-mile trip to Piseco for the purpose of fishing off Fall Stream Bridge. To aid in conservation efforts, Fall Stream was declared closed to fishing from 1919 to 1922.

William B. Abrams was issued a license to operate a dance hall on May 18, 1928. His amusement center was located at the head of the lake on Old Piseco Road. Visiting band members would be provided overnight accommodations in the loft of the barn located behind the dance hall.

Ice cream, sodas, and Cracker Jacks were popular treats offered inside William B. Abrams's dance hall. Also for sale to visitors of the establishment were cigars, beer, candy bars, and postcards. In addition, the dance hall was equipped with pinball machines and a nickel slot machine for the amusement of the summer tourists. Abrams routinely entertained guests, calling square dances on Saturday nights at the pavilion.

The open space adjacent to the dance hall was used as an aircraft landing field in the 1920s and 1930s, as well as an athletic field, where the town baseball team competed against other nearby towns. This property is now the location of Half Moon Beach, a private campground. Old Piseco Road and Rudeston Mountain can be seen in the background.

In 1930, William B. Abrams, a worker at the famed Sacandaga Amusement Park, purchased a Dentzel Carrousel from his employer. Abrams installed the merry-go-round at his Piseco Lake campsite. The carrousel was manufactured by Gustav Dentzel, a German cabinet maker who established a factory in Philadelphia in 1860. The unit featured hand-carved wooden horses made from poplar and bass and was powered by a steam engine. In the late 1940s, Abrams sold the property and the new owner removed the carrousel, which is preserved today at the Shelburne Museum in Vermont.

Influences of Native American culture can be seen throughout the Adirondacks. Native linguistics have been used to identify countless features across the region. Primitive artifacts have been discovered at various sites at Piseco Lake, some dating back 4,000 years. The trail marker shown in this photograph was located near Abrams's dance hall and identified, for the benefit of tourists, a fabled old Native American trail running between the towns of Morehouse and Wells.

Clyde's Restaurant was operated by Clyde Diedrich and family from 1944 to 1958. The business also rented out cottages located on a hill behind the restaurant. This log structure stood east of the airport and burned down in 1958. The cottages were then moved to the beach area known as Golden Sands.

The Diedrich family operated Golden Sands, a seasonal tourist business located at the head of Piseco Lake. The property contained approximately 20 cottages, a lodge, tennis courts, a restaurant, and a long stretch of sandy beach. This aerial photograph shows the beach and tourist cottages at Golden Sands in the 1950s. Silver Lake is visible in the background.

District No. 1 Schoolhouse, located in Upper Rudeston near Silver Lake, was built in 1890. The new school contained a large central potbellied stove, wallpaper, and a pump organ. After the tannery closed, the population shifted to Piseco Village and the school was converted into a private residence.

This 1940s photograph, taken from the top of Rudeston Mountain, shows the old Tannery House and Tavern owned by Hugh Riley. Piseco Lake and Silver Lake can be seen in the distance. The local tannery, which operated in this area in the late 1800s, was named Silver Lake Tannery. The first telephone line running to the Piseco area was installed at the tannery in 1898.

Riley House, built in 1850, is one of the oldest buildings still standing in the town of Arietta. During the bustling days of the tanning industry, the building served as a dormitory for the workers of Silver Lake Tannery. The house came into possession of local farmer Hugh Riley, who also operated his saloon next to the house. The building is now the home of the Piseco Lake Historical Society.

In the late 1800s, when the logging and tannery businesses were at their peak, Hugh Riley operated a saloon in Upper Rudeston. Local taverns bustled with activity as workers socialized while quenching their thirst. With the decline of the tanning industry, the saloon slowly fell into disuse. From 1905 to 1909, the building served as the Rudeston Post Office. The tavern can be seen in its original location before being relocated to the other side of the Riley House in the late 1950s. (Courtesy of the Abrams family.)

By 1956, the Riley House and Tavern were owned by Molly Rockwell. Rockwell restored the original 19th-century bar in the Riley Saloon to aid in its preservation. Standing in the taproom today, one can imagine the dim lighting and tobacco haze as thirsty tannery workers and loggers enjoyed the warmth of the potbellied stove while partaking of their favorite spirits. Twelve saloons once lined the road between Piseco Village and the Lake Pleasant town line.

CAMPING AT LAKE PISECO - 1933

Over the years, scouting groups have visited Piseco Lake for camping, hiking, and boating activities. This group of young campers from the Frankfort Boy Scout Troop participate in outdoor whittling projects at their camp at Piseco Lake in 1933.

Dreamland Pavilion, built by Hugh Donahue in 1938, offered customers ice cream, beer, gasoline, and weekly entertainment. In 1944, the Piseco Fish and Game Club purchased the building after its foreclosure. The pavilion was used as a meeting hall and offered various forms of community recreation, including roller-skating. The Piseco Fish and Game Club donated the building to the town in 1971 for use as a community center.

Rudeston Post Office, as it appeared in 1912, stood in the vicinity of the Silver Lake Tannery on Old Piseco Road. At this time, three separate communities—Lower Rudeston (Higgins Bay), Rudeston, and Upper Rudeston—were named for the Eli Rudes family, who were among the first settlers in the region. Rudeston Mountain rises behind the building to the right.

Due to low-lying wetlands, a long causeway was necessary to travel from Lake Pleasant Road to Upper Rudeston and Piseco. At the end of the causeway, a bridge was built over Oxbow Lake Outlet. This view of Oxbow Lake from the outlet bridge has changed little in 90 years.

The schoolhouse for Arietta School District No. 2 was built in 1851 in the Higgins Bay area. The land for the school had been purchased from George Warren and Henry Vail of Troy for $1. Classes were held in this building for 55 years. In 1906, a new schoolhouse was built in the approximate vicinity and still stands today.

Over the years, this area carried several different names, including Rudeston, Lower Rudeston, and Spy Lake. It was finally renamed Higgins Bay on April 1, 1938. The white building with the hip roof is the Spy Lake Schoolhouse around 1908.

After Arietta Road (Route 10) was rerouted, this stretch of road near Higgins Bay was renamed in honor of Wayne Smith who served in the U.S. Army during the Vietnam War. Smith was killed in action in 1968 at the age of 21.

116

Nine

DAYS OF INDUSTRY
AND AGRICULTURE

In the late 19th century, Arietta, which had relied on agriculture, was revitalized by a variety of industries, including tanning, spruce gum picking, tree tapping, and even gold mining. Lumbering was the dominant industry, as the vast forestlands attracted numerous logging companies. These companies sent scouts, or cruisers, into the abundant forestlands to select the location of lumber camps, as shown above. Logging operations began after harvest season and continued through winter. Oxen and horse teams, rented from farmers, removed the massive logs from the forest with the assistance of large wooden sleds.

In the 19th and early 20th centuries, farming was a necessity for Adirondack families. Isolated communities located far from markets needed to be self-sufficient and grew fruits, vegetables, and grains. Fodder was also grown to feed farm animals, such as horses and oxen, which were needed to power plows and reapers. Arietta resident James Higgins readies his team of oxen, named Buck and Bright, for a long day's work near Piseco Lake.

A local farmer prepares to harvest his crop of hay or oats with a mechanical reaper on a field near Higgins Bay. Adirondack farmers found little need for steam-powered farm implements being used extensively in less mountainous regions. Farmers in the Piseco area contended with rocky top soil, short growing seasons, and cold weather, making cash crop farming nearly impossible.

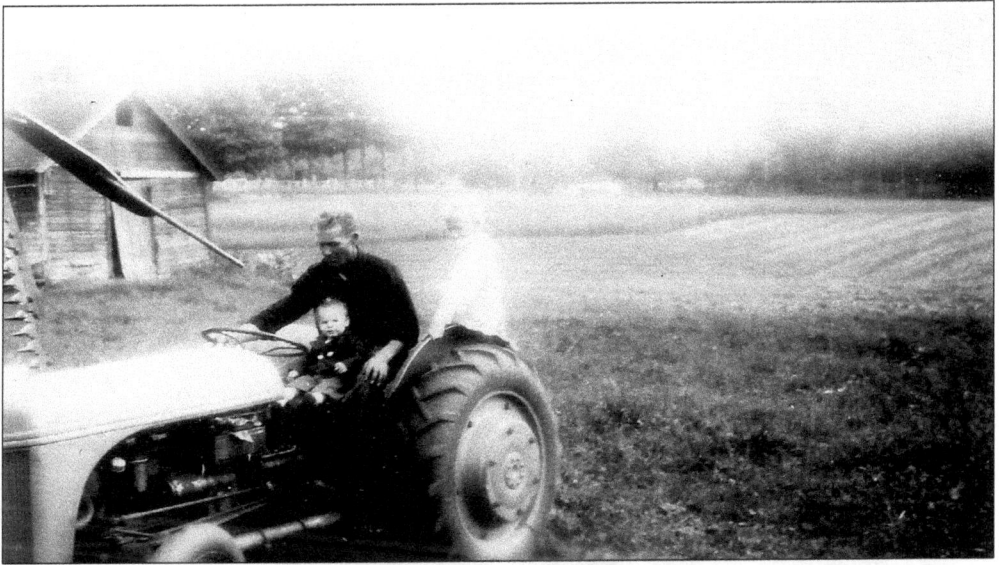

Since farms were small in the Piseco area, the need for self-propelled mechanized farm machinery was limited. A tractor and its accessories found favor among people who were still farming the land in the 1940s. Tractors were also used in logging operations, road repair, and to power other labor-saving devices. Pictured are members of the Higgins family riding a tractor used to harvest hay.

Farmers commonly found employment during the winter months working in lumber camps throughout the Adirondack forest. This temporary occupation was extremely dangerous, as loggers could be crushed by falling trees or injured by heavy sleds, nicknamed "go-devils," used to remove logs from the woods. This group of lumbermen at the Old Flow lumber camp around 1900 display tools of their trade, such as jam pikes and a peavey. The camp was located at what is now known as Evergreen Lake in Arietta.

Small lumber camps were located throughout the forests in Arietta during the 19th century. This bark shanty in the deep woods served as a camp kitchen and dining facility for lumbermen. Since good food was constantly on the mind of the hardworking loggers, they were eager to know the names of the cooks before signing on to a shanty. Women at lumber camps were a rare sight and were usually wives of cooks or foremen.

Many years ago, the lumber industry was common throughout Arietta. Logs were processed into planks in local sawmills or were floated downriver to larger mills. The west branch of the Sacandaga was a minor highway used during river driving operations. Pictured is a sawmill located in Rudeston along Lake Pleasant Road (Route 8) around 1900.

Well into the 20th century, Adirondackers relied on burning wood to provide home heating. The effort needed to fell a tree with an ax or crosscut saw was a daunting task. Logs needed to be cut into usable lengths, split, transported, and stacked. In the 1930s, companies began producing economical machines easily handled by the consumer. Pictured are residents of Piseco in the 1940s operating a gas-powered saw to produce firewood.

The Old Mill, Piseco Lake. N. Y.

In 1835, land around Piseco Outlet was purchased by Solomon van Rensselaer as a location for a sawmill. Water emptying from the lake provided a power source for the mill. Van Rensselaer's Mill sat on the northeast bank of the outlet and was used to process lumber and manufacture clothespins, washboards, tool handles, and piano parts. The mill was operated by a number of proprietors and gradually fell into disuse. The mill burned in 1968.

Piseco Lake Outlet House N.Y. July 5, 1913

Across Arietta Road from the Outlet Mill stood the Mill House. The Mill House was originally part of the van Rensselaer milling complex and was used for manufacturing operations. This structure also served as a residence for the mill workers and was infamous for being infested with bedbugs. The Mill House, then owned by the International Paper Company, was burned due to road construction in 1967.

Early sawmills relied on moving water to power machines that processed lumber. If the water did not move at the proper speed, a dam was created to facilitate the movement of a large waterwheel. This wheel, connected to a series of shafts and belts, provided mechanical energy to the mill. A group of visitors stand by the dam at the Piseco Outlet Mill not long after its construction in 1888.

Logs were pulled from the water and placed on a carriage that carried the logs to the moving saw. Sawmills used vertical muley saws and circular rotary saws to cut the logs into boards. The processed lumber would then be stacked and air dried to remove moisture. This seasoning process could take up to three years to accomplish. The wood was then ready to be manufactured into a desired product or sold to builders and craftsmen. The Piseco Outlet Mill was also a production center for individual wood products that were distributed to businesses in larger cities. This photograph shows a series of rollers attached to the mill's floor used to transport lumber throughout the building. The cone pulley (below, center) would have been used to change the speed of the leather belts and machines connected to the apparatus.

Sawmills were in operation in Piseco as early as 1827. Large-scale lumbering began after the Civil War as lumber camps and sawmills dotted the area. Pictured is Enos Murphy's Old Flow lumber camp at the beginning of the 20th century. In 1910, an outbreak of smallpox forced the camp to be quarantined. A sawmill continued to operate at this site into the 1930s.

In Upper Rudeston, the stone foundations are all that remain of Silver Lake Tannery, which closed in 1900. Tanneries were located near hemlock trees as the bark was needed to transform animal hides into leather. Soaking the hides in hemlock liquor resulted in a pliable leather. The leather was transported to Gloversville and Johnstown and manufactured into various products. As hemlock became scarce and chemical processes developed, the importance of tanneries decreased.

Early settlers believed the rugged Adirondack Mountains contained precious metals and minerals. In the 1850s, the Belden brothers dug a mine shaft near Spruce Lake in search of gold. They worked the mine in secrecy for years, bringing barrels of ore through Piseco Village in the dead of night en route to the rail station in Amsterdam, New York. Many people still wonder if the secluded mine was indeed actually producing gold. (Illustration by Steven N. Nassiff.)

Before modern refrigeration, wooden iceboxes were used to preserve food. Ice from the lake was cut with a saw and removed with ice tongs or by a mechanical conveyor. Each block, weighing up to 300 pounds, was loaded on a sleigh or truck and carried to an icehouse, where it was carefully packed between layers of sawdust for preservation throughout the summer months. Shown are members of the Abrams family cutting ice on Piseco Lake. (Courtesy of the Abrams family.)

Tapping maple trees in the early spring to produce maple products was an important source of income for Adirondack residents. Larger sugar bushes in the region contained over 50,000 trees and yielded thousands of pounds of maple sugar and syrup. Floyd W. Abrams managed a small sugaring operation behind his Sportsman's Home on Haskell's Road in Piseco. Snowshoes were needed to navigate the deep winter snows during tapping season.

Tim Crowley, pictured at his camp at Spruce Lake in the late 1800s, was a local woodsman and guide who earned a living for 25 years picking spruce gum. During the winter, the gum was scraped from trees with a sharp file attached to a long pole. After a harvest, the chewing gum was processed and wrapped in Boonville. Each pack carried the label "Pure Adirondack Gum" and sold for 5¢. Pickers received $1.50 per pound of gum. (Courtesy of the Piseco Lake Historical Society.)

This small rocky stream, which feeds Piseco Lake on its northern shore, was named Mill Stream for the industrial mill once situated on its banks. The stream was used to provide power to the mill during the 1800s. The remnants of the mill can be seen in this 1920s photograph. Various types of mills had operated in the Piseco area, such as sawmills, shingle-making mills, gristmills, and machine shops.

By the late 1800s, industrial activities began to affect the natural environment of the Piseco area. Large tracts of land had been denuded of trees, and soil erosion altered the landscape. A dam built at the outlet mill increased the water levels in Piseco Lake and its outlet, drowning sections of forestland. The area pictured is now referred to as Big Bay, and water levels are still controlled by the dam at the outlet bridge. Over the years, nature has reclaimed the area's magnificent beauty, luring generations of visitors to Piseco Lake.

Visit us at
arcadiapublishing.com